The Divorced Catholic's Guide to Parenting

The
Divorced Catholic's
Guide to Parenting

Lynn Cassella-Kapusinski

Our Sunday Visitor
Huntington, Indiana

Nihil Obstat
Msgr. Michael Heintz, Ph.D.
Censor Librorum

Imprimatur
✠ Kevin C. Rhoades
Bishop of Fort Wayne-South Bend
January 6, 2020

This book is not intended to replace the advice of psychologists or other healthcare professionals. It should be considered an additional resource only. Questions and concerns about mental health should always be discussed with a healthcare provider.

Our Sunday Visitor Publishing Division
Our Sunday Visitor, Inc.
200 Noll Plaza
Huntington, IN 46750
www.osv.com
1-800-348-2440

ISBN: 978-1-68192-380-2 (Inventory No. T2265)
1. FAMILY & RELATIONSHIPS—Divorce & Separation. 2. RELIGION—Christian Living—Family & Relationships. 3. RELIGION—Christianity—Catholic.

eISBN: 978-1-68192-381-9
LCCN: 2019956580

Cover design: Tyler Ottinger
Cover art: Shutterstock
Interior design: Chelsea Alt

PRINTED IN THE UNITED STATES OF AMERICA

This book is dedicated to all the parents and children who have opened their hearts to me, especially my own parents from whom I have learned the most.

Contents

Introduction

Perhaps you have seen research regarding the higher divorce rate for children from divorced families, as compared to those from intact families, and worried about whether your child will be able to beat the odds. You may feel overwhelmed about the prospect of helping her as well, given the weight of your own grief, plus the added stress that your divorce or separation has likely brought you. You may be wondering, how do you start to help your child adjust and heal? And keep on helping her? How can others assist you with this daunting task? Will all these efforts really make a difference?

This book will help you answer these questions, plus encourage and affirm you as a divorced or separated parent. That is the good news: You can definitely make an appreciable, positive difference in helping your child embrace this cross and grow stronger from it, both personally and as a Catholic. It will not be easy. However, this book is designed to give you a very practical, step-by-step road map for getting started. It also weaves in important tenets of the Catholic Faith in providing essential guidance, grounding, and wisdom.

I include my experiences as a Catholic child of divorced parents as a teaching tool throughout this book. These experiences provide an in-depth, intimate look at what your child may be thinking, feeling, and struggling with, but either is unable or unwilling to share with you because of not wanting to add to your difficulties. I also share personal experiences of the healing and growth that results when trying to be a good disciple carrying the cross of divorce as a child. In this way, I share with you a "double vision," an intimate view of this struggle from a child's eyes and the perspective of a woman who was fortunate to grow from these wounds and get marriage right, as a result of God's grace, the sacraments, and devoted family members. I hope what I share here will reassure you that your child can also experience healing and growth with these vital supports.

I have never been divorced. As such, I cannot offer direct experience as a divorced parent in providing guidance. Nor is this book designed to be a co-parenting resource or to help you, specifically, with your personal healing. (There are many excellent resources already available to help you in those regards. Please see the appendix.) Instead, I will share my professional expertise in counseling divorced or separated parents. I will also share my parents' struggles as divorced parents and what they did well and not so well from my perspective as a child on the receiving end of their parenting.

I have written this book because I know intimately, as a child of divorced parents who has beaten the odds, the critical role that faith plays in helping one carry this cross and allowing it to shape us in ways that are healthy and holy. I also know how necessary Catholic teachings are in providing wisdom and guidance in this process. This journey is simply too difficult and tricky for children to navigate otherwise, no matter how favorable the circumstances. In order to arm your child with these necessities, you must first be armed with them, as your child's most important teacher and role model. This is a demanding task to be sure, especially when grappling with your own divorce grief. I encourage you to take the time to care for yourself and get extra personal support. It will strengthen you to be the best parent you can be for your child, who will remain much in need of your guidance and support throughout this journey.

I speak from experience. I was eleven when my parents separated and sixteen when they divorced. Shortly after the separation, my father moved away and, eventually, across the country. I visited him during the summers and holidays, and we kept in touch through letters. More than anything, I wanted him to be an active and regular part of my life. It did not happen in the ways I needed, causing me to feel abandoned for many years, even though I had a very devoted mother and an older brother who looked after me like a father. I tried to fill that gaping hole through achievements and, later, by seeking the approval and affirmation of other successful men like my father, but to no avail. It was only when I mustered the courage to enter into my wounds and accept this cross in my life with God's help and the guidance of the Church that I grew stronger. I was then able to learn from the lessons in my parents' divorce and allow them to motivate me to get marriage right. I was able to beat the divorce odds because I clung to God and the Church as critical parts of the solution.

Another major part of the solution was my parents. They responded to me in ways that helped my healing significantly. They also responded in ways that hindered my healing. Why is your involvement as a parent so crucial? First, as your child's most important role model, she will look to you first and foremost to learn what to do with her grief. Your reaction will either encourage her to own and process her feelings about the divorce or send them underground where they are likely to do more damage. Handling these feelings in a healthy way requires certain helping skills, which I will teach you. Children also need to learn skills for communicating and solving divorce-related problems constructively, and your example will either help or hinder them. This book will help you there, too. Your relationship with your child will likely strengthen as a result of these efforts, and you will experience relief and joy in the process.

My parents' divorce was tough, but it brought me closer to my family members. It also helped me grow in ways that I would not have grown otherwise, because of the challenges I was forced to wrestle with and overcome in order to find peace. I mention this not because I am pro-divorce, but to emphasize what Saint Paul writes in Romans 8:28: "We know that all things work for good for those who love God, who are called according to his purpose." As overwhelming as divorce can be, we know by faith that God is good. We can draw strength from God and his purpose for our lives when we accept the cross that befalls us in divorce.

Your Catholic Faith will also be a critical part of this journey of helping your children heal and grow. You may feel alienated from the Church right now because of her teachings on divorce. If so, remember that divorce, in itself, is not a sin (I address this in more detail in chapter 12). Or, you may be wrestling with difficult questions such as how a good and loving God could allow the divorce to happen to you and your children. If you are feeling distanced from your faith, I encourage you to find a priest, pastoral counselor, spiritual director, or Catholic support group with whom to process these questions and feelings. These interventions can make a profound difference in your healing and put you on more secure emotional footing.

I do not think lasting healing and peace after divorce is possible for children or parents without God's help, as this experience is too overwhelming, even if the divorce affords relief from negatives such as destructive parental fighting, as it did in my case. Church teachings also help significantly, even if they seem to set the bar too high. In this book, I will hope to help you better understand those teachings as they relate to divorce situations, and, in turn, share them for your child's benefit.

This book is designed to accompany you as you seek to guide and support your child. Throughout these pages, you will find important instructional information, practical suggestions, and, at times, research findings. I will not overload you with academic information. I promise. Instead, I will provide what you need to know to help your child, including Catholic teachings so you can benefit from the Church's rich wisdom and be supported fully. I will also share parts of my personal journey as an instructional tool, which may shed light on your child's experience. Each chapter is divided into the same sections for your quick reference: My Personal Sharing and Orientation to the chapter topic; Practical Suggestions; Meaningful Connection Time with Your Child; What the Church Says; Thorny Situation(s); and Questions for Reflection.

Healing and growth are possible for your child after your divorce. But children need adult intervention to achieve that healing. Time alone will not heal their wounds, nor will the loving support of a stepparent rid them of their grief. Even if you find a good pastoral counselor to help your child with this journey, I encourage you to use this book as well to learn more about your child's grief, how to address it constructively, and ways to manage problems that may arise as a result of your divorce or separation. As a parent, you will influence your child the most. Consider using that influence to affect him in positive, healthy ways on this journey. You may even find your own healing and growth nurtured in the process.

This book will not address every issue you will face as a divorced or separated parent. Rather, it is meant to help you find a foothold in the Catholic Faith and psychological principles. The book is divided into five main areas:

- Chapters 1–3 address emotional impacts that divorce or separation may have on your child, corresponding challenges for you as a parent, and concrete applications for addressing those challenges, plus the guidance of Church teachings.
- Chapters 4–7 present common problems children

have as a result of co-parenting difficulties and/or a parent's personal problems, how to avoid and communicate constructively about them, and the importance of taking proper care of anger.

- Chapters 8–9 highlight how to help children bring God and forgiveness into the solution and integrate the guidance of Church teachings.
- Chapters 10–11 explore circumstances that result in the later stages of divorce if a parent dates and/or remarries, and how to use the divorce as a teaching tool about the Sacrament of Marriage.
- Chapters 12–14 help you help your child if the other parent is absent or if you are an absent parent, and provides guidance on enlisting outside resources for additional support.

There is a building process to this book with the topics in chapters 1 through 9. Whether you are using this book to work individually with your child or as part of a psychoeducational group program, those chapters are designed to go in sequential order, if possible. This is because your child will need to get her bearings emotionally and cognitively before being ready to grasp the catechetical aspects of this journey.

You can certainly read this book for your own individual use as well. You will find some concepts and pieces of my personal story repeated throughout. This is because of their importance and in case you want to refer to a specific chapter, when needed, instead of reading the chapters in consecutive order.

I sincerely hope this book helps you gain understanding of your child's perspective and needs, learn how to help her in a holistic manner that treats faith and Catholic teachings as essential to the solution, and experience peace and joy in drawing closer to your child and seeing her grow stronger not in spite of, but through this difficulty.

May God bless you and guide you on this journey.

CHAPTER ONE
Helping Your Child Adjust to a New Sense of Family

When my parents separated, it felt like my family had been hit by a massive cue ball in a game of pool. It broke us apart and scattered us in different directions. We withdrew emotionally from one another in trying to cope with our feelings. The exception was my older brother, Marc, who often discussed the many changes with me, as well as our thoughts and feelings about them. Our conversations brought us closer and gave me a strong sense of family. It taught me that family means coming together to help one another as best one can, especially in times of difficulty.

I did not talk much about the separation with my parents, though, and felt distanced from them as a result. With my mom, it felt like a taboo subject because it, understandably, got her upset, so I avoided it. My dad often raised the topic, but only to share his remorse and regrets or irritation with how my mom had treated him during their marriage. He treated me, in essence, as a confidant not as a child who needed help adjusting to the divorce. I sensed that he very much needed me to take on this adult role, so I supported him as best I could, ignoring my own questions.

This lack of communication with my parents about my concerns made me feel like I did not have a "real family" anymore. It also reinforced my sense that I could not ask them for help in making sense of the changes. I did not feel I had permission to express my thoughts, feelings, needs, and desires. My relationships with my parents also lacked clear boundaries in terms of my helping them. In the end, we all did the best we knew how to do at the time, but we operated without the help of counselors, priests, friends, or support groups. I had to figure out on my own how to think of my family and my role in it, facing the limitations and losses involved. Most importantly, I had to accept that my family would not fit my ideal for how a family should operate and accept that God had a bigger plan for me through this hardship. Your child may be experiencing a similar struggle, especially if focusing only on outward indicators or what he observes about other families. He may be perceiving that other families are perfect or have no problems because, on the outside, things look fine.

Your divorce or separation will challenge your child to broaden and deepen her understanding of family. In order to grow in this regard, she will need to focus on and appreciate what is most essential, namely love, commitment, a willingness to forgive, empathy, and so on. She will also need to forgo her needs at times, when adjusting to the realities of one parent not living all the time with her, a parent moving on and establishing another family, and many other changes and losses that accompany divorce. Many divorcing parents with whom I have worked have also had difficulties accepting the loss of their family as they once knew it or hoped it would be. In efforts to deny the pain of that loss, either for themselves or their children, some plead with the other parent to continue spending holidays or doing recreational activities together, usually at the request of their child who is sad that they do not do anything as an intact family anymore. Other parents may be in a serious dating relationship and looking to replace their child's family with one that includes only their new partner, excluding the child's biological parent as if tossing out a pair of old shoes that no longer fit.

Neither approach serves children well, however. The first approach prevents children from grieving the losses and accepting the reality that the divorce is final and their parents will not be getting back together. The second approach, when parents fail to recognize and accept that the other biological parent will always be part of their child's family no matter what, does serious damage to the child's sense of self and can foster deep-seated resentment. No parent has the right to jeopardize their child's relationship with the other parent. This is important, and I will repeat it throughout this book. Moreover, if parents truly want to foster their child's healing, they will do all they can to foster the child's love and forgiveness of the other parent.

The goal for you as a parent is to strike a balance between these approaches. On one hand, it means helping your child grieve the losses associated with no longer having an intact family (see helping skills in chapter 2, beginning on page 41). It also means helping your child acquire a new sense of family and realize that he still has one, even though it has changed. Children also need to be taught that there is no such thing as a perfect family, because every family, no matter how flawless they appear on the outside, is comprised of imperfect persons. Your child will also need your support in acquiring and adjusting to his new sense of family. This means respecting that your ex-spouse and his or her relatives may still be included in your child's family, despite your different relationship with these persons.

Practical Suggestions

The following suggestions can help your child maintain a sense of family during divorce or separation.

1. Try to establish a regular pattern of contact with your child and, in particular, between your child and the parent who has moved out.

The more predictable the contact with each parent, the better it will be for your child. While your ex-spouse's departure may not have come soon enough for you, this departure can easily create anxiety, worry, and fear in your child about losing their other parent "for good." Remember that your child needs and remains dependent on both you and his other parent. Knowing when and how often he will be seeing each of you will provide him with stability and reassurance that he can still count on the love and support of both of you despite other changes.

2. Provide an emotionally safe environment in your family.

Emotional safety means that your child can state her thoughts, feelings, and desires freely, without fear of being reprimanded, shamed, or dismissed. Not providing this environment will distance your child from you and jeopardize her grieving in the process. (For practical guidance in this regard, see helping skills in chapter 2, beginning on page 41.) Children need to be instructed that their feelings are not wrong or sinful, but what they do in response to them can be. They should not be reprimanded for having feelings; instead, they need to be taught how to control and express their feelings in healthy, respectful ways by your example.

3. Do not violate boundaries by using your child as a confidant.

It may be tempting to confide in your children and rely on them for support as you deal with your own hurt and anger from the divorce. This is especially tempting if your children are older or willing to listen. You may think this sharing is not causing harm and even view it as a way of maintaining open lines of communication. However, from your child's perspective, while he may want to know the information, he lacks the maturity to process it. As a result, and especially given his dependence on you as a child, he may take on the role of confidant and see it as his responsibility to help you get through the divorce by listening to your problems and concerns. This is a highly inappropriate burden to place on a child. It adds to their stress, encourages them to disown their own grief, and, as a result, postpone their healing. For your child's sake, maintain clear boundaries and seek outside support to help yourself process and heal from the divorce. Consider individual counseling and/or an adult divorce support group. (See chapter 14 and the appendix for resources.)

4. Do something together as a family on a regular basis.

Carving out regular time to spend together in your "new" family in each household can be especially difficult when juggling schoolwork, extracurricular activities, and more as a single parent. However, it is particularly important to establish this routine for your children so they continue to feel connected as a family, especially when so much is changing for them as a result of the divorce or separation. This routine can include activities as simple as having meals together and saying prayers at bedtime. It can also include attending Mass, then going out to eat and, perhaps, doing a family or volunteer activity together. Another weekly activity that children enjoy is a Friday pizza and movie night.

Children also need one-on-one time with you, as well as exclusive time with their other parent, during this transition. This time, again, can be spent doing something simple together like playing a game or reading a story together, and if your child wishes, it could be a time when she can raise any divorce-related concerns privately with you.

5. Consider visiting relatives on a regular basis as well, including your ex-spouse's relatives.

Especially after your divorce, if these relationships are amicable, it can be very supportive for children to continue visiting relatives on both sides of your family. This contact can further reinforce for your child that she does, indeed, still have a family. I greatly appreciated spending time with my father's side of the family after the divorce. It always helped me feel close to my dad, who was living across the country, and learn more about his upbringing, which gave me further insight into who he was as a person. I enjoyed these relationships before my parents divorced, and appreciated them even more afterward.

6. Maintain consistent family routines as much as possible.
Routines are important for children, especially children experiencing divorce or separation, because they help them feel safe and secure by knowing what to expect. Try to keep routines (e.g., mealtimes, bedtimes, visitations with their other parent, etc.) as regular as possible. If a routine will be changing (for instance, if you are moving to a new neighborhood or sending your child to a new school), give your child ample advance notice so he can prepare for it by asking questions and, if possible, be involved in small decisions regarding it.

7. Maintain firm, consistent discipline and limits.
Perhaps you have become lax with discipline and limits because you feel guilty and do not want to be too tough on your child given all she is going through, or you may simply lack the energy. In either case, however, those limits are precisely what your child needs. They will help her feel more in control, and equally important, they will keep her from using the divorce or separation as an excuse for doing poorly. This is also particularly important for her success at school. If you are "enabling" your child at home, she will likely expect her teachers to do the same, or at least conclude she won't get in any real trouble, because you are not giving appropriate consequences at home.

By the same token, "catch your child being good" also. Positive recognition is the best way to shape behavior, so try to praise it when it happens.

8. Pray daily with your child.

Your child will learn to pray primarily by watching you. Let him see and hear you talking with Jesus like a best friend. In addition, find a regular, daily way to invite your child to pray with you as well. It can include common times such as before meals and/or at bedtime. However, consider other innovative ways also, such as when driving in the car, by writing a letter to God, or through drawing, coloring, or painting. Remember to praise God from your heart when something good happens and ask your child to pray with you when he is sad or worried about something. In short, let your child know there are many different ways to pray and reassure him that God will listen whenever and however he chooses to do so.

9. Practice gratitude regularly.

A good way to start is by thanking God for the blessings in your lives and specifying what they are. Ask your child if he would like to highlight these ideas creatively by creating a gratitude space in your home and/or keeping a gratitude journal. The space can be a small desk with supplies and thank you notes as well as a place that everyone in the family can use for placing small, surprise thank you gifts for one another. Or it could be a gratitude window that is decorated and changed with the seasons or holidays. Let your child hear you thanking God out loud for the good things that happen to you in the course of a day, as well.

10. Talk with your child about the struggles of the Holy Family.

It can be very helpful to use the Holy Family (Jesus, Mary, and Joseph) as an example of families getting through hardship together. Mary and Joseph faced numerous challenges, including Jesus' birth while they were traveling for the Roman census and fleeing from Herod while Jesus was an infant. Remind your child that God supported them through those trials because they trusted and reached out to God in faith. God can do the same for your family also!

Meaningful Connection Time with Your Child

When talking with your child about family, try to reinforce these points:

1. **Perfect families do not exist.** No matter how good a family looks on the outside, it is not perfect. This is because all families are comprised of imperfect persons.

2. **All families experience losses and difficulties.** While your family is experiencing the hardship of divorce or separation, another child's family may be grappling with the death of a loved one, a parent's unemployment, mental or physical health problems, military deployment, and so on. Everyone experiences crosses in this life, both as part of a family and as individuals.

3. **Family members show love in different ways. Love is what makes a family.** We all have different strengths and weaknesses that affect our way of loving others. We need to be open to appreciating the different ways in which our family members show their love and accepting their limitations in this regard also.

4. **The Fourth Commandment requires children to honor their parents** (Ex 20:12; Dt 5:16). This respect also flows to brothers and sisters (CCC 2219). In addition, it includes honor, affection, and gratitude

toward the extended family. It also means obeying other authorities, such as teachers.

What the Church Says

The Church is clear in her instruction regarding the duties of parents. As a child of divorced parents, two teachings in particular strike me as highly relevant. First, the Church tells us "parents must regard their children as children of God and respect them as human persons" (CCC 2222). This includes respecting your child's relationship with his other parent, not undermining it with negative and angry comments based on your own experience, which may not be relevant. Some parents bad-mouth the other parent in attempts to get their child on their side. Others do it because they fear their ex-spouse will only hurt their child as he or she has hurt them. My mother bad-mouthed my father for this reason. While her intention was to protect me, I resented the negative comments because, after all, this was not just any man to me. He was the most important man in my life, whom I loved and who was part of me. My mother's attacks against my father felt like attacks against me, and they drove a wedge between me and her. The comments also did not serve any constructive purpose. While my father had his shortcomings, he was a much better father to me than he had been a husband to my mother.

Another very helpful Church teaching is that "everyone should be generous and tireless in forgiving one another for offenses, quarrels, injustices, and neglect. Mutual affection suggests this. The charity of Christ demands it" (CCC 2227; Mt 18:21–22; Lk 17:4). Your child may be very upset with his other parent regarding a divorce-related injustice and refuse contact for this reason. Sometimes, of course, it is necessary to cut off contact when a parent is dangerous or physically or emotionally abusive, a topic which I address later on. While it is important to affirm your child's feelings and help him set appropriate, self-respecting boundaries with such a parent, it is also important to remind him that, as Christians, Jesus says we are to place no limits on forgiveness.

Your example, of course, is critically important in this regard. If your child sees you working toward this same goal, he will be much more likely to incorporate it as his own. It can also be helpful to remind your child that neither he, nor you, know the full story about why a person acts in a certain way. Only God knows the full story and, as such, is best qualified to determine justice. Thus, we need to leave justice in God's hands. No matter how fragmented our family, we are called, as Christians, to do what we can to help rebuild and strengthen it.

Thorny Situations

Cohabitation of Other Parent

You may be wondering how to approach the situation of your ex-spouse's dating partner with your child, especially if your ex is in a cohabiting arrangement with this partner. Does this situation mean you should have a discussion about chastity and sexuality with your child sooner than you were planning? If so, how can you address the co-habitation in an age-appropriate manner that upholds your Catholic values and morals without bad-mouthing your child's other parent?

For Catholic guidance on these questions, I recommend starting by reading "The Truth and Meaning of Human Sexuality (TMHS): Guidelines for Education Within the Family" from the Pontifical Council for the Family. It is easy-to-read, thorough, and can be accessed for free via the official website of the Holy See.[1] In this document, the council offers encouragement to you as a parent, stating that you are "in the best position to decide what the appropriate time is for providing a variety of information" when it comes to sexuality.[2] It adds that "the most intimate aspects, whether biological or emotional, should be communicated in a personalized dialogue" with your child.[3]

There are also Catholic resources available to help you, especially if your child is not attending a Catholic school where this information may likely be addressed. These resources include RCL Benziger's K-8 Family Life program, *Beyond the Birds and the Bees: Raising Sexually Whole and Holy Kids* by Gregory and Lisa Popcak, booklets published by the Catholic apostolate Family Honor, and *Theology of Her Body/Theology of His Body* by Jason Evert.

You may also have concerns that exposing your child to your ex's cohabiting situation may jeopardize the Catholic morals that you are trying to instill. While a possibility, in my work with divorced families, I have found that a parent's example of chastity and clear communication of this value outweigh this risk. I also experienced this firsthand. When I was a young teen, I visited my father when he was living with a woman to whom he was not married. At first it was uncomfortable for me, as my mother had always instilled in me the teaching that couples should not live together before marriage. As a Catholic, I knew cohabiting was not a good or right thing to do. My main concern when visiting my father, however, was my own relationship with him, not his relationship with his girlfriend. As I grew older, my father's cohabiting situation reinforced my beliefs in the Church's teaching

---

1. The Pontifical Council for the Family, "The Truth and Meaning of Human Sexuality: Guidelines for Education within the Family," accessed October 17, 2019, Vatican.va.

2. Ibid., No. 65.

3. Ibid., No. 66.

on this issue, as I did not see positives resulting from it. I could not say he was happier or more at peace as a result of the cohabitation.

Dishonorable Other Parent

The Fourth Commandment says to "honor your father and your mother, that your days may be long in the land which the Lord your God gives you" (Ex 20:12, Dt 5:16). However, how can your child do that if her other parent has abandoned or done something intentionally cruel to her such as physical or verbal abuse, or cutting off financial support for taking the other parent's side? Does this commandment still apply to your child in these circumstances? I have worked with children in this situation who have mistakenly claimed it does not.

Before getting to practical applications of the commandment in these circumstances, I think it is helpful to arm children with the Church's stance in response to evil in general. Saint Paul tells us, "Do not be conquered by evil, but conquer evil with good" (Rom 12:21). The intent is not to "defeat" the evil person, but to defeat the action done to us by walking in the goodness of God. It means making a choice to do good despite the wrong done to us. Why should we encourage children to aspire to this higher goal? Because that is how to prevent another's evil from overcoming God's goodness in them. This goal focuses them on staying open to the good that God wants to do in them, and not surrendering to the evil as a victim. In short, by honoring a dishonorable parent, your child grows in becoming a person of honor himself.

What might this look like in practical terms? First, it is important that your child understands that she needs to honor herself in this process. This means maintaining healthy, self-respecting boundaries that keep her safe emotionally, physically, and so on. Once she understands and accomplishes that, help her consider these ideas for honoring her dishonorable parent:

- Pray for this parent and ask God to help him become

a better person.

- Ask your child in what ways have others treated this parent honorably and to consider doing the same.
- Model respect for your child's other parent and speak to him with kindness.
- Seek to understand this parent's weaknesses, including what past hurts may be contributing to his current behaviors.
- Look for the good in the other parent and thank him for whatever good he may have provided or taught your child.

Infidelity of the Other Parent and/or Your Infidelity

In general, I suggest that you do not broach the topic of infidelity unless your child knows about it and raises it first. Children are already grappling with so much in the wake of the divorce that adding to their stress by involving them in one more negative aspect, especially one they lack an adequate frame of reference for, does them no good. If your child asks you a direct question about the affair, though, you need to be truthful. Some parents assume they can lie and keep the affair a secret. However, not only is that unlikely, but when your child discovers the lie, it will erode his trust in you and make it that much easier for him to lie to you in return.

As with other adult aspects of your divorce, remember to share only basic information, not the sordid details. For example, "Your father (or mother) does not want to be married to me anymore. S/he has decided that s/he prefers someone else." As your child gets older, if you can present the infidelity in a larger context that puts responsibility on both you and the other parent and helps your child learn information to apply to his own relationships, that is ideal. For example, "The infidelity occurred when your father was under a lot of stress at work. He did not think I would understand. I was busy with my own job at the time and did not make an attempt to understand. He began going to the bar and drinking to cope with his stress, and we moved farther and farther apart." Your child will appreciate your efforts to take the "high road," and not use the transgression as an opportunity to bash his other parent (and, thus, your child himself) in the process.

Questions for Reflection

1. What am I willing to do (or stop doing) to help give my child a stronger sense of family?

2. How have my childhood experiences of family influenced what I am instilling in my child about family?

3. What Church teachings explored in this chapter do I agree with? Are there any I do not agree with? If so, why not?

CHAPTER TWO
Understanding Your Child's Grief Journey and How to Respond to It

Ialways knew my father would leave one day. My parents' fighting had gotten too destructive and had gone on for too long. I did not want my father to leave, but I needed the fighting to end. The only way that seemed possible was for them to separate physically. My mom later told me, when I was a young adult, that my dad took me aside to tell me he was moving out, but I have no recollection of it.

Their separation set in motion layers of loss that took me over a decade to heal from. My father soon moved across the state and then, eventually, across the country. We kept in touch by letters and visits during the summer and holidays, but he was not a regular part of my life. My mother also drifted away from me as she grappled with her grief. I would find her napping on our family room couch when I arrived home after school and spending appreciable time alone in her bedroom with the door closed. She had never done those things before. I began to worry a lot about her ability to survive the divorce emotionally. I already felt emotionally abandoned by my dad, and I was terrified of the same thing happening with my mom. Because of my dependency on her, I could not focus on my own grieving because I knew she was having difficulties emotionally.

I did not know how to handle my worry and sadness. I needed to find a way to lessen the power those feelings had over me, so I turned to my schoolwork and extracurricular pursuits. Making straight A's and winning awards was one thing I could control, and I clung to those pursuits like a life preserver. It distracted me from my grief and turned my fears, sadness, and worry into feelings of success. My victories lifted my mother's spirits and gave me assurance that she would not be destroyed by the separation. These pursuits also helped me feel as though I was doing something to earn my father's love. If I could achieve enough, I reasoned, I would get my dad to notice and show him that I was worthy of his love.

It can be easy to deny divorce grief as a child, because in most circumstances parents remain alive; in a child's eyes, this means the possibility exists for their parents to get back together. This absence of finality makes divorce grief a unique type of grief for children. In order to support your child in working through it, it is critical to understand some tenets along with your indispensable role in this process.

Grief Principle #1: Children's feelings need to be acknowledged in order to be healed.

As difficult as it is to see your child hurting as a result of your divorce or separation (something you may feel you could have prevented), it is critically important to let your child experience the pain. It may seem counterintuitive; however, the more children can sit with the pain and accept it, the more readily they can move through it. You may think that allowing your child to feel sadness or anger will only cause those feelings to intensify and, perhaps, overpower her. But the reverse is true: Acknowledging feelings helps your child move through them and make room for other feelings. It boils down to helping your child accept the reality of her situation. Just as we care for physical wounds by cleaning and dressing them, so we must tend to children's emotional wounds in an attentive and loving way.

What I am proposing is difficult to do, especially when your child's hurting stirs up your own grief. In your desire to help your child (and you) feel better, you may respond by reasoning her feelings away, sugarcoating reality, or telling a white lie. You may think these actions cause no or little harm, but in the long term, they will thwart her healing because they send her incorrect messages about grief and encourage her to disown her feelings.

Unfortunately, there is no way to bypass the fact that your divorce or separation results in a loss for your child, regardless of any positive changes. Perhaps you fear your child will not be able to bear the pain. If so, remember that children, like us, have defense mechanisms that buffer them from feeling the full weight of their grief until they are ready. These mechanisms are similar to an air bag in a car that protects our bodies from the physical impact that could kill us. After the impact, the airbag needs to be stuffed back into the module so we can drive the car. Your job as a parent is to respond constructively to your child as she moves through that journey of putting that air bag back into place — on her own time and in her own way as she is ready.

Realize that your child's questions and the expression of her pain, even when it tears at your heartstrings, are moments to be celebrated, as they signal that she is moving through grief. It's far better to do that sooner than later, when those losses may grow in number and possibly leave your child feeling angry, depressed, or removed from her feelings altogether.

Grief Principle #2: Your response to your child's grief greatly impacts whether or not he will own it or push it away.
When learning how to handle their grief, children take cues

from the adults around them. Your child will look to you first and foremost in this regard, so it is critical that you respond in a way that lets your child know he has permission to express his feelings and is not weak or wrong for doing so. It is not wrong to have feelings. Having feelings is part of being human. Jesus certainly had and expressed them, as we learn in the Gospels. For example, when approaching the tomb of his friend Lazarus, "Jesus wept" (Jn 11:35). When entering the temple in Jerusalem and seeing how it was changed into a market, Jesus became so upset that he "made a whip out of cords and drove them all out of the temple area, with the sheep and oxen, and spilled the coins of the money-changers and overturned their tables" (Jn 2:15).

My mother had a difficult time whenever I expressed negative feelings about the divorce and, in particular, missing my father. She would point out that other kids had it worse than I did (which was true), or she would criticize me for "not being stronger." Although she wanted to help, her response taught me to be ashamed of my feelings and to view myself as weak, inferior, and "bad" for having them. Not only were these conclusions in error, but they also encouraged me to disregard and disown my feelings and, as a result, become stuck in grief.

I have worked with other parents who take a more passive approach, denying that divorce results in a loss for their child. These parents will focus on the ways in which the divorce hasn't changed anything for their child. Perhaps their ex-spouse was not home much because of work commitments. On the other hand, they may argue that the divorce has resulted in a better situation for their child because the other parent is finally spending more time with the child. Neither of these arguments is fair to the child. No matter what, divorce results in a permanent change for the child and, as such, represents a loss. We also know that divorce is not what God intended, as God designed the marital relationship to mirror the love between Christ and his Church. No matter how slight or positive the change, it is not "natural" for a child's parents to live apart as separate entities, cut off from each other. The child remains part of each of his parents and, as such, experiences the breaking of their bond as a division within his very self.

The more you can help your child acknowledge and own his grief, the better it will be for his healing. See the "Practical Suggestions" section later in this chapter for specific helping skills that you can use to help your child process his feelings.

Grief Principle #3: Children are unique, and their way of grieving and their timetable for healing will also be unique. Children do not grieve like adults do. Instead, they grieve intermittently. They may cry one minute when thinking about the divorce, then want to go out to play the next minute. Given their development level, they will likely need more indirect ways to express their feelings and thoughts about the divorce. For example, your child may prefer to draw her feelings, thoughts, and experiences, write about them in a journal, express them through a song, or work with a counselor. Encourage whatever she wants to try. Whatever the outlet, help her get into a regular routine of using it, so this way of caring for feelings is repeatedly reinforced.

I also encourage parents to consider family counseling as a preventive measure. Not only do counselors have skills to help children process their feelings and thoughts more fully, but children often share more with an outside adult. With a parent or a teacher, children have the added worry of disappointing the adult and/or being evaluated for a grade. They are freed from this worry with a counselor. In addition, it is helpful to have a counselor as a check-in person as your child gets older and experiences other divorce-related changes such as a parent dating, remarrying, moving out of the family home, and so on.

Also remember that your child's wounds are likely to heal at a much slower rate than yours, given her developmental needs and the tricky nature of this loss for her. Your child will rework and process this loss at higher levels as she matures. She is also likely to revisit her wounds as she experiences other milestones and big events, such as graduation, prom, and the like, as well as other changes that may occur in your family.

There is no set timetable for children's healing from divorce. The grief really never ends. Instead, children become better equipped to move through it as they mature. The key is to approach their grieving in a healthy manner that will allow them to integrate the losses in their lives in a growth-filled way. I learned more from my parents' divorce than any other experience in my life. It also served as a powerful motivator for me to get marriage right. Similar benefits can result for your child, too.

Grief Principle #4: Children experience uncertain losses in divorce, which make them more challenging to resolve.
Children do not experience divorce losses as final losses. That is because, for them, while something is lost, something is also still there. For example, a parent moves out of the home, so a child may not see that parent as much. That same parent may start dating or become overwhelmed by personal problems, either of which takes attention further away from the child. Yet, the parent remains a parent, and the child is left alone in determining what that role now means. Even in situations where the nonresident parent becomes more attentive, the nature of the child's relationship with that parent still changes and, as a result, contains elements of loss. When situations remain uncertain like this, children cannot grieve the losses associated with them.

I was stuck in grief for many years because of the ambiguity in my relationship with my father. This uncertainty was intensified by our irregular contact and my not knowing him very well. He did write me letters, but they were primarily vehicles for expressing his feelings and struggles, not to make a connection to my feelings or enter into my world. As a result, I remained unsure of what I could expect from him, especially with him living so far away. In essence, I was confused about what it meant for me to have him as my father. Could I still turn to him for advice and guidance? Would he still be there to help me find my way in the world? If he was not able to provide this support, would that change in the future? I was unsure how to answer these questions and, as a result, was stuck in emotional limbo for a long time.

The more clarity that your child achieves regarding the divorce losses, the more she will be able to grieve them and move on. This boils down to helping your child understand what is lost and what remains the same.

Grief Principle #5: While divorcing parents are grieving the death of a relationship, children continue to need both parents involved in their lives.

Your child's task in divorce is very different than yours with respect to your ex-spouse. You are faced with the challenges of grieving the death of a marriage and forming a "business partnership" with your ex-spouse (in terms of raising your child well). Your child's task is the opposite, however: He continues to need as close a relationship as possible with your ex-spouse as well as you. While you are disengaging emotionally, your child needs to stay engaged emotionally with your ex-spouse.

You must accept and respect this fact, which is not at all easy, but so necessary. Otherwise, you will inadvertently harm your child's functioning, healing, and future ability to form and sustain a healthy marriage. As the old adage goes, you need to "love your child more than you hate your ex."

Grief Principle #6: Parents need to respect their child's grief journey as separate from their own.

I have worked with many parents who are unwilling to separate their grief journey from their child's journey. Often, this manifests in a parent's unwillingness to take control of anger. The vast majority of their actions are made in response to anger, and they refuse to take the high road of personal discipline. These parents may seek to erase the other parent out of the child's life just as they seek to erase their ex from their own life. This is a grave error and one that does a major disservice to your child, adding to her grief and stress because she will feel pressured to take sides. Your child's relationship with your ex-spouse should be free to exist on its own merits without your interference. You do not have the right to damage your child's relationship with her other parent. Such an action will only add further burdens for your child.

No matter how dishonorable a parent, that parent remains part of your child forever by virtue of the fact that he or she helped to bring your child into existence. This, of course, does not mean ignoring boundaries with a parent who may be indifferent or cruel, or not protecting your child from an abusive relationship. However, when possible, it does mean helping your child get to know her other parent and the reasons why that parent may be absent from her life. (See chapter 10 for further guidance.) If it is a situation of abuse, you can still help your child understand her other parent and what factors might have contributed to abusive behavior. This prevents your child from blaming herself for the situation and keeps her from harboring anger and bitterness. It can also pave the way for empathy and forgiveness later on, which will foster healing and peace.

When a divorced parent tries to erase their ex-spouse from their child's life, it affects the child. This is often seen in the school setting. Some children become confused about whether or not to write their father's last name on their papers. Some feel as if they do not have permission to talk about their fathers or mothers and, instead, have to profess love for their mom's new boyfriend or dad's new girlfriend. Others act out their internal conflict at school by not doing their work, not eating, or being highly disrespectful to teachers. Children need both their parents, especially as they solidify their own identities. Give your child freedom to live her own journey. It will end up nurturing your relationship with your child as well.

Developmental Needs Impacting Divorce Grief

Your child's grief journey will differ significantly from yours because of the lack of clarity involved. Your child's developmental needs will also have a direct bearing on his progress through grief. According to Jean Piaget, a Swiss psychologist known for his work on child development, children from the ages of seven to eleven or twelve are in the "concrete operational" stage of development. In this stage, they can reason logically, but their reasoning is tied to specific or concrete situations or objects. As a result, they typically focus only on the outside signs of their parents' problems or what they can observe, but they are unaware of deeper tensions between parents. For example, they may think the reason their parents divorced is simply because of name-calling, or always being mad at each other.

Children this age may engage in magical thinking also, like younger children. For example, they may think they have the power to bring their parents back together if they behave in a certain way. I had magical thinking about my father's involvement in my life. I thought that if I achieved enough I would be able to make my father love me in the ways I needed. It is more consoling for children to think they have this unrealistic power than to realize that, sometimes, bad things happen in the world that they cannot control.

Children this age tend to think in extremes as well. For example, they may view one parent as "mostly good" and the other as "mostly bad," which can encourage them to take sides. They may view their life in black-and-white terms as well, where everything is perfect one minute, then totally bad as soon as a setback comes along.

Around age eleven, children typically start to move into the "formal operational" stage of cognitive development. This is when most young people are able to go from specific observations to broad generalizations, allowing them to think conceptually and abstractly. This allows them to reflect on concepts such as love and heaven and abstract issues of cause and effect. They may wonder if they caused the separation or a parent's lack of involvement in their lives. Unlike younger children, however, they may not be as willing to share these thoughts. Their higher level of cognitive development also allows them to come to abstract conclusions about their parents' behavior. It also allows them to acquire a deeper grasp of religious concepts.

Around age eleven is also when children typically start to turn to peers for support. They may become protective of a parent, especially one who is not doing well. They may take on the role of the absentee parent by caring excessively for younger siblings as well.

Preadolescents, particularly boys, may become aggressive as a way of releasing their inner conflicts and tensions. For example, they may provoke a classmate or get into other trouble at school. They may become subtly aggressive toward you as well, especially if they feel safe with you and assured that you will not leave them. This may include refusing to do chores or behaving like their other parent just to irritate you. Engaging in conversation with boys is so important because talking it out can reduce their acting out.

Preadolescent girls usually respond differently. Instead of being outwardly angry or sad, they may focus on being overly helpful and attentive to parents. By doing this, they can experience what the late Judith Wallerstein, a psychologist and pioneer in divorce research, termed the "sleeper effect."[4] When this happens, their repressed anger, fear, or other emotions that were delayed at the time of parental breakup bubble to the surface later in adolescence or young adulthood when they enter dating relationships.

Finally, it is not uncommon for children to go through a period of regression during separation or divorce. This means

---

4. J. S. Wallerstein and S. Blakeslee, *Second Chances* (Independently Published, 2018), 59-67.

they may start to act like a younger child, wetting their pants or the bed, becoming overly dependent on a parent, or playing with stuffed animals. If your child is regressing, know he is not doing this on purpose. Instead, it is often a child's way of going back to an earlier, safer time in their lives as they try to manage their stress.

Practical Suggestions

1. Get personal support for yourself and move forward as best you can.

In order to support your child's grief work, it is critically important to get personal support for yourself. The more in touch you are with your own feelings and can manage them, the better you will be able to help your child. According to researchers, one of the best predictors of children's functioning after divorce is the psychological adjustment of the resident parent along with quality of parenting provided by that parent. Children's adjustment is typically no better than that of their resident parent. Your child needs to sense that you are okay in order to feel she has freedom to focus on herself.

Be good to yourself and consider joining a divorce support group and/or seeing a counselor. (See the resources noted in chapter 14 and the appendix.) The extra support can nurture not only your grief work, but also your steps in building a new, healthy life for yourself.

2. Be willing to focus on your child's inside story.

This suggestion may require you to take a new outlook toward your child. As a busy and stressed parent, your focus may be, understandably, on compliance and getting things done for your child, meaning you are focused largely on his external behavior. While that focus is important, it is also necessary to pay attention to his inside story or the reasons why he may be acting in a certain way. Even though you may think you know why your child is behaving in a particular way, check it out with him. Often, conclusions can have more to do with what is going on inside of you as the parent. This orientation to your child will help him honor his feelings and feel better about himself, and it will strengthen your relationship with him.

Empathizing with your child in this way when you are also grieving is difficult work, but it is worth doing. Remember, as a parent, you are your child's primary role model and, as such, the way you respond to his feelings will greatly affect whether he owns grief or pushes it beneath the surface, where it can do more damage. While it may be very difficult to hear your child's feelings, realize you will do him a world of good by letting him express them. Read on to learn how to do so.

3. Place a check on your empathy.

We know that empathy plays an important role in fostering closeness in our family relationships. It also helps your child's wellbeing and can bring personal benefits for you. However, like many good things, balance needs to be maintained so you do not neglect your own feelings and needs in the process. Otherwise, research shows that empathy can take a physiological toll on you.[5]

How can you achieve a healthy balance when empathizing with your child? One of my graduate counseling professors shared a helpful orientation with my class years ago. He said, "You cannot help if you are part of the train wreck." My understanding of that powerful image is that it is important to maintain some distance when empathizing. Thus, in the process of trying to understand what your child is thinking and feeling, and in the midst of your concern about her suffering, it is necessary to regulate your empathy. This means placing a check on

5. Erika M. Manczak, Anita DeLongis, and Edith Chen, "Does empathy have a cost? Diverging psychological and physiological effects within families," *Health Psychology* 35, no. 3 (March 2016): 211–218.

it so you do not live in that space and lose your sense of self and your ability to help. It helps to hold onto the hope — the improvement, well-being, and happiness — that awaits your child precisely as a result of embracing the struggle.

4. Show acceptance of your child's feelings with helpful responding skills.
As a parent, you can show acceptance of your child's feelings by saying something like "That sounds very difficult" or "What was that like?" Those are helpful responses. Just be sure to match the words with a sincere, open, and attentive tone of voice.

Unhelpful responses are ones that stifle or minimize your child's pain. Some examples are, "At least your father is still alive" or "You should be stronger than this." Hear the difference? Unhelpful responses send children the message that certain feelings are "bad" and that the child is "bad" for having them. As a result, children learn to repress their grief.

Specific Strategies

Name the feeling you see or hear. Simply notice how your child looks or her tone of voice, and give words to her feelings. An example is "You look really sad" or "I can hear your voice shaking." Naming provides a wonderful invitation for your child to explore her feelings.

Restate what your child has said. Restatements are a repeating or paraphrasing of the substance, content, or meaning of what your child has said. These restatements typically have the following characteristics:

1. They contain fewer but similar words.
2. They are clearer and usually more concrete than your child's statement.

3. They can be phrased either tentatively or more directly.
4. They refer to things your child recently said.

Suppose, for example, your child says he does not like that his father is now living in a small apartment where he does not know any of his neighbors and does not have a dog. You could respond by saying something like, "It sounds like you are worried about your dad being lonely since he is living by himself in a new area." This example actually goes further because it includes a naming of the feeling also.

Mirror feelings. You can use this strategy when your child has stated feelings, or when you can infer your child's feelings based on something they have told you. For example, suppose your son says, "I was so mad I punched the wall and hurt my hand." You could respond by saying, "You were furious."

Some tips for mirroring feelings:

-   Use the word "you" to reflect back the feelings you have heard.
-   Focus on the main feeling and perhaps the reason for that feeling. For example, "You feel _____ because _____." This is important, as children can tell you about five different feelings in the course of five minutes. You cannot mirror them all, so choose the one you feel may be most important.
-   Stay at this level. Do not interpret or offer an explanation from your perspective. Otherwise, the focus of the conversation will shift onto your thoughts and feelings, instead of keeping it on your child's inner experience.
-   Check for accuracy, especially when feeding back a long communication. For instance, "Do I understand you properly?" or "So, what I think I hear you

saying is _____. Is that right?" This assures your child that he is heard, and it ensures that you understand what has been said.

- Finally, stay sensitive to how much reality your child can handle at any given moment. You can threaten your child by prematurely mirroring feelings that he experiences difficulty in acknowledging. Also, keep in mind your child's cognitive level and the limitations that go along with it.

Give small verbal rewards. Small verbal rewards are an easy, effective way to let your child know you are listening. Examples include: "Uh-hum." "Sure." "I hear you." "Tell me more." "Really?"

Use open-ended questions and probes. Like us, children can get confused and stuck when describing their difficulties. Questions and probes help them clarify them as well as think about different aspects of their problems. They also demonstrate that we are listening and interested. Open-ended questions usually begin with "what" or "how" and thus prevent a young person from giving one-word answers. "Why" is also an open-ended question, but I recommend avoiding this one, as it can put your child on the defensive. You can also phrase your probe as a directive, such as "Tell me more about that" or "Give me an example of what would be helpful."

5. Model the behavior that you expect.

As mentioned, your child will take cues about how to handle grief largely from you. If your child sees you minimizing your own grief, making excuses, or blaming others for difficulties, she will learn to do the same.

Demonstrate how to take responsibility for difficult feelings. One way is to share your day-to-day feelings with your child. This, of course, does not mean letting her see uncontrollable expressions of rage or weeping, or burdening her with details. Rather, it means admitting you are sad, angry, or feeling guilty. This sends your child the message that it is okay to admit feelings, and that those feelings do not have to overwhelm her. Your child very much needs this guidance and will look to you to learn how to grieve in a healthy way.

Meaningful Connection Time with Your Child

When talking with your child about grief, try to reinforce these points:

1. Grief is like waves or a roller coaster ride.

Tell your child that his grief feelings may go up and down like waves in the ocean or a roller coaster ride. For example, suppose your child's father has moved out, but he drives your child to school or sports practice. He may feel sad after his dad drops him off, and his grief goes up. Then, after getting busy with classes or an athletic drill, his grief may go down. When arriving home, he may see a picture of his dad in his room or a sibling may talk about him, and his grief may go up again. Grief waves are normal and do not mean he is going crazy.

Another helpful image is that of a symphony. For me, my parents' divorce has been like a symphony that is always playing. Sometimes the music crescendos or gets louder. Other times, the music decrescendos or decreases in volume.

If your child does not express much in terms of feelings, you may want to speak with him about feelings he might experience in the future, emphasizing that all are normal parts of the grieving process. This may help him feel more comfortable sharing his feelings with you and others in the future.

2. Grief can be confusing.

Let your child know it is normal if she feels two different feelings about a situation. This is common for a lot of kids (and adults). For example, your child may feel happy that the fighting has stopped or lessened because of the separation, but sad because she is missing the parent who has moved out. It can be uncomfortable to have two different feelings, but the more your child expresses and talks about them, the better she will feel.

3. Grief can affect the body.

Instruct your child that feelings can cause changes in his body also. For example, if he is worried, he may feel a pain in his stomach. If angry, his muscles may tighten, his face may get hot, and/or his heart may beat faster. Let your child know that, if this happens, he can take a short break to pay attention to his feelings and get in touch with what they are telling him. This may help him feel better and can alleviate worries that he is getting physically sick.

Grief can show up physically in terms of interruptions to your child's typical sleeping and/or eating patterns also. You know your child best. If the interruptions go on for too long or become severe and concern you, be sure to contact your pediatrician.

4. There are healthy and unhealthy ways to express grief.

We often forget that children are a valuable source of information regarding their experiences. Ask your child what she would like to do to get her feelings out. Help her consider constructive options, such as writing her thoughts and feelings in a journal; drawing; writing a note to God; praying; talking or playing with a pet; listening to music or playing an instrument; ripping up newspaper; punching a pillow; and so on.

Also let your child know what she does not have permission to do when upset. This could include yelling, slamming doors, throwing papers, overturning furniture, or taking emotions or feelings out on someone else by aggression toward you or a sibling. Be sure to discipline your child should she engage in what she knows not to do!

For guidance during the school day, see chapter 14.

What the Church Says

In doing the hard work of supporting your child's grief journey, it helps to stay grounded in Church guidance on this topic. The Catholic Church teaches that "passions, or strong feelings, are good when they help us do something good, but evil when they encourage us to do something wrong" (CCC 1768). Some psychologists go so far as to state that a well-balanced emotional life is necessary for growth in virtue as, otherwise, our ability to freely choose good is hindered.

The first step to help your child adopt a proper orientation to his emotions and feelings is to assure him that they are not sinful. He need not be afraid of them. To the contrary, they are a gift from God. However, like all gifts, he needs to use them responsibly. He needs to engage his reason and will so he can act in a morally good way as a result of them (CCC 1767). No matter how intense and painful, your child can direct anger, sadness, and other difficult feelings toward something good with God's help, the graces of the sacraments, and proper guidance regarding grief. As Saint Paul tells us, "All things work for good for those who love God" (Rom 8:28).

Thorny Situation

When Children Will Not Talk about the Divorce or Separation

Depending on your child's developmental level and the stressors associated with your divorce or separation, he may require displacement techniques in order to express his inside story. As an indirect form of communication, these techniques provide children with a nonthreatening way to talk about emotionally charged issues. They include vehicles such as books or movies, drawing, and using puppets, dolls, or action figures. These vehicles are also effective because they are familiar to children and engaging for them.

Reading books or watching movies about divorce with your child can be particularly effective, because they help him put a frame around his experience. By identifying with a character, your child may be better able to articulate his own thoughts and feelings. These vehicles can also support him in asking questions that may reveal concerns he is having, but is reluctant or unable to share more directly.

A children's psychoeducational group program can also be very beneficial. Groups provide children with a feeling of safety through numbers. This can greatly facilitate their expression of feelings, often allowing this expression to happen earlier than it does in individual or family counseling. For more information about divorce groups for children, please see chapter 14.

Questions for Reflection

1. What do I find most difficult to do when trying to support my child's grief journey?

2. How would I rate the job I am doing from 1 to 10 (with 10 being the best)? Why?

3. How can I allow the Church's teachings on emotions to shape my response to anger or other difficult feelings so I can be a better example to my child?

CHAPTER THREE
Explaining the Divorce or Separation to Your Child and Why It Matters

My parents did not talk with me about why they were separating. It was something I knew would happen eventually, as their fighting had gone on for too long and was only getting worse. As an eleven-year-old, I did not understand much about relationships, and I knew even less about their possibility to improve even after years of destructive fighting and other negatives. I assumed the only way to make the fighting stop was for my parents to divorce and asked no questions about it. Because I was a preadolescent, my focus remained concrete. I was preoccupied with how my parents were doing emotionally. I needed them to survive the breakup so they could still parent me.

During the years that followed, each of my parents told me separately about the reasons for their marital problems. Their feelings were still (understandably) raw, so their explanations contained many disparaging comments about each other. Nevertheless, I listened and tried to make sense of what went wrong and why they could not work things out. As I got older, however, I wanted to know more about what caused my family foundation to crumble, and why this damage happened to those whom I loved most.

In addition to impacting their ability to progress through grief, children's developmental level also impacts their understanding of why parents separate or divorce. As mentioned in chapter 2, children from ages seven to eleven or twelve are in the concrete operational stage of development, during which their reasoning is tied to what they can directly observe. They are further limited by their lack of life experience. For example, young people this age have told me they want to know why their parents argue and are mad at each other and cannot "forgive and forget" like they have done with a sibling. Young adolescents (ages twelve to fourteen) have similar limitations as a result of their narrow life experience and maturity level. For example, they may conclude that their parents divorced simply because they did not try hard enough. Or the higher cognitive development level of young adolescents may lead them to ponder more abstract questions such as what their life would be like had their parents not divorced. One defining characteristic that researchers have found in children this age is their ability to judge each parent and his or her behavior as an individual.[6] However, given that young adolescents typically lack an understanding of their parents' perspective, they often react in anger and express harsh moral judgments of their parents.[7]

Children need relevant information and guidance to understand the separation or divorce accurately and feel more secure.

---

6. C. Springer and J. S. Wallerstein, "Young adolescents' responses to their parents' divorces," New Directions for Child and Adolescent Development, 19 (1983): 15–27.
7. E. A. Anderson, "An exploration of a divorce statute: Implications for future policy development," Journal of Divorce, 12, no. 4 (1989): 1–18.

However, they may not air their questions because they do not want to upset their parents or themselves, as discussing the topic often brings hurt feelings to the surface. Thus, they tend to stay silent and fill in the gaps on their own, often with incorrect details. This means that you, as the parent, will need to take the first step in addressing this topic. It is not possible to do it perfectly, nor can you prevent your child from experiencing pain in the process. However, with advance planning and God's grace, you can have an honest and loving conversation that will help him understand on an age-appropriate level why the divorce or separation is happening.

It will take your child time to understand and accept the reasons for your divorce or separation. Remember that while you may have been processing this decision for months or years, your child has not. Being at a less advanced stage of development and maturity will necessitate her need for more time to process this reality as well.

Catechetical instruction will be an important part of helping your child grow, of course. However, realize that this instruction must come at the proper time, after your child has gotten her bearings emotionally and cognitively. Otherwise, she will not be ready to receive it. Much like an air bag that needs to be deflated and put back into place before one can drive a car, so too does your child need to absorb the loss sufficiently before she is able to apply Catholic teachings and move forward with her growth on this level. When your child is ready for this next step, please see chapter 12 for guidance.

Practical Suggestions

1. Start the divorce conversation early and revisit it as your child matures.

While it may be uncomfortable, raising this topic lays a critical foundation because it sends your child the message that he has permission to talk and ask questions about the divorce or separation. And you have confidence in his ability to handle these discussions.

He will need this permission not only at the outset, but for many years ahead. This is because children rework divorce losses and process them at higher levels as they mature. In addition, your child may need to discuss divorce-related changes in the future, such as a parent dating or remarrying. Your child's own personal transitions, such as graduating from high school or getting a first job, may be more emotionally charged for him and necessitate more discussion as well. This is because these changes can aggravate the grief associated with your child's prior losses. It is important to keep in mind that every loss is a multiple loss.

Timing will be important when initiating that first difficult conversation. Wait until you are prepared for what to say and can say it calmly. Remember, it is okay to show some emotion and model this for your child; however, you want to keep your emotions under control. This will show your child that you can take care of yourself in the midst of the changes, which means you will be able to take care of him, too.

Your child may quickly become overwhelmed during these conversations, so keep in mind this rule also: the shorter and simpler the explanation, the better. Do not allow your need for processing to spill onto your child. I once worked with a very polite ten-year-old who was quick to obey anyone in authority. This included serving as a sounding board for his mother as she shared her feelings and fears as a result of her separation from his father. The boy told me the information made him sad and confused to the point where he had appreciable difficulty sleeping. Even though your child may seem more mature or is willing to provide a listening ear, remember he remains a child and, as such, needs you to continually set appropriate emotional boundaries.

Even if your child does not say anything in response, your initiation of the topic will help to normalize these communications going forward. Rest assured, when your child is ready to share his thoughts and feelings or ask questions, he will do so. Setting aside this private time will also nurture your child's trust in you and reinforce for him the feeling of "we will get through this together."

A parent once told me her son did not have any questions regarding the separation because he was not asking her anything about it. As I got to know her, she shared that she was very uncomfortable raising this topic and, as a result, did not. While it is important to follow your child's lead (as will be mentioned in suggestion #4), it is also important for you to initiate this topic and provide some general instructional information regarding it. Even if your divorce does not come as a surprise to your child or he has friends whose parents are divorced, do not assume your child does not have questions. What is more likely is that he does not feel he has permission to talk about it and/or fears that doing so might upset you.

For more guidance on this topic, see "Meaningful Connection Time with Your Child."

2. Repeatedly remind your child that she is not responsible for the breakup.

Many children wish for their parents to get back together and will hold on to that wish until a divorce is finalized. One of the most difficult psychological tasks for children is accepting the permanence of this situation, especially given that both parents typically remain alive.[8] This wish can encourage children to try and get parents to reconcile. This can happen in the school setting, for example, where a child suddenly starts to have academic problems, hoping it will bring her parents back together as they try to solve them. Children need to be reminded repeatedly

---

8. J. S. Wallerstein, "Children of divorce: The psychological tasks of the child," *American Journal of Orthopsychiatry*, 53, no. 2 (1983): 230–243.

that the divorce or separation is a grown-up problem; as such, nothing they said or did caused it, and conversely, nothing they say or do can fix it.

3. Give your child freedom to avoid eye contact.

Children often talk more freely when not having to make eye contact. If your child is having difficulty communicating about your divorce or separation, try having these conversations when driving in the car or playing a game with him. One mother told me the best conversations she had with her son occurred right before he went to bed at night when the lights were turned off. The more you can free your child to talk, the better.

4. Let your child lead.

If your child will not talk with you about the changes, it may mean she is not ready to. There is a limit to how much reality we all can handle, especially children. Your child could also be silent because the situation makes her sad and/or because she does not want to risk learning that the divorce is definitely going to happen.

Give your child permission to talk and ask questions when she is ready. Let her lead you. Do not nag or pressure your child, even though knowing what is on her mind may, understandably, help you feel better. In the meantime, simply let her know on a regular basis that you are open to talking whenever she would like to.

If your child is a young adolescent or older, know that she may be more likely to ask questions. This is because, as mentioned earlier, children this age have an increased ability to judge each parent and his or her behavior as individual.[9]

5. Consider seeking professional help.

If you are unaccustomed to exploring feelings in your family or simply need extra help and support in talking with your child

---

9. C. Springer and J. S. Wallerstein, "Young adolescents' responses to their parents' divorces," New Directions for Child Development, 19 (1983): 15-27.

about the divorce or separation, consider enlisting the help of a family counselor. The counselor can serve as a bridge that fosters healthy communication between you and your child, and help with raising awareness of your blind spots that may be getting in the way. See chapter 14 for more information on this resource.

Meaningful Connection Time with Your Child

1. Explain what divorce or separation means, even if you think your child knows. If possible, discuss the topic with your child's other parent present.
A good way to begin this discussion with your child is to approach it on a teaching level by giving a brief explanation of what separation or divorce means. See below for suggestions on what to say, based on your child's age. With older children, another option is to begin by asking them what they think separation or divorce means, then clarify any misconceptions. Once your child has an adequate understanding, spell out how the change will impact him with the information that has been agreed on so far. The nagging question on your child's mind will be: How will this affect me? So, be as clear as possible in answering it. Stick to the facts and be direct.

What to Say

- **Example for Separation:** "Your dad/mom and I are having a lot of trouble getting along. We need to live apart for a while so we can figure out if we can solve our problems and how to do so. The problems are between your father/mother and me. You did not cause them. We still love you very much and will always take care of you."

- **Example for Divorce:** "Divorce is a legal process that

parents go through when they no longer want to be married because they are very sad together and have serious problems that they have been unable to solve. These problems are between your father/mother and me. You did not cause them. We will always be your parents and will always love and take care of you."

- **With older children:** "I'm sure you know that your father/mother and I are having a lot of trouble getting along. Unfortunately, we have been unable to solve these problems and need to separate/divorce. These problems are between your father/mother and me. You did not cause them. We will always be your parents and will always love and take care of you."

- **Tell your child what will and will not change in their lives.** Give as many specifics as possible regarding matters affecting them. For example, "Your dad/mom will be moving to Grandma and Grandpa's house. You will still see him/her, but it will be on Wednesdays and every other weekend. We will still be living in our house, and you will still be going to the same school, etc."
- **Ask your children if they have any questions or concerns.** However, do not pressure them. Let them know they can ask questions or share concerns at any time.
- **For questions you cannot answer:** Simply say, "Your dad/mom and I do not know yet, but we will figure it out, and let you know."

2. Do not raise the topic of "love" or other adult topics.
While it may be true that you and your child's other parent no longer love each other, do not share this adult detail with your child. It will only add to your child's confusion. Moreover, he will likely become concerned that you and his other parent may

stop loving him, too. Children and adolescents do not have the maturity nor the experience with romantic relationships to realize how the love between a parent and child differs from that between married adults.

On the other hand, some parents may look to lessen the impact by telling their child that they and their ex-spouse are still good friends and just "grew apart." However, that also does more harm than good for two reasons. Again, in having no experience or understanding of how adult relationships are different, a child cannot grasp what "growing apart" means or the reasons for it. Second, from a child's perspective, if nothing really bad happened between you and their other parent, they will likely conclude that you had no sufficient reason to divorce.

3. Avoid blame. Instead, own your part when discussing the divorce or separation.

Your efforts to take the high road and avoid blaming your child's other parent will have an appreciable, positive impact on your child. She will take note of it and appreciate the respect shown her. It also serves as a powerful way to be an influential role model, which she will carry with her always.

Your child, on the other hand, may be looking to affix blame, given her developmental level. Nine- to twelve-year-olds tend to have a rigid sense of morality, which can influence them to pick sides and pass judgment on parents. Sometimes, they take sides because it helps them feel more in control emotionally as well. Along these lines, your child may also be curious about "who divorced whom." Young adolescents have the capacity to think on a higher level and, as a result, may become highly critical of a parent's behavior.

Given these tendencies, it can be helpful to share with your child your part in the circumstances leading to the separation or divorce. Again, this does not mean giving a lot of personal details. Rather, the intent is to address the roadblocks that may arise between you and your child, especially if you are the parent your child perceives as being the more responsible party, or the one who made the decision to leave. It also shows that you value being honest with your child, just as you expect her to be with you. For example, if you are the one who filed for the divorce, you may want to consider sharing this fact with your child.

My father shared with me that he was the one who decided to separate and, later, file for divorce. He also explained why he moved so far away after the separation, which was what I most needed to know since it had a direct bearing on how often I could see him. Fortunately, he shared this information with me and did so by accepting full responsibility for the decision. His honesty drew us closer and prevented me from coming to inaccurate conclusions that would have added considerably to my hurt.

What the Church Says

During these discussions with your child, it is helpful to keep in mind Church teachings regarding the Most Holy Trinity as they give an important orientation when references to your child's other parent arise. We know that God is Trinity, a communion of the three divine persons, Father, Son, and Holy Spirit. The Christian family is a sign and image of this same communion (CCC 2205).

What can easily be forgotten, however, is that this life of the Triune God remains in your family, even though the family as you and your child once knew it is breaking up as a result of divorce. Your child will continue to have an innate love for you and his other parent, a love that remains inseparable from his own life. Just as the Holy Spirit originates from the love of the Father and the Son for each other, so too is there a mutual love between not only your child and you, but also your child and his other parent. That mutual love should not be jeopardized by the hurt and anger that you may have toward your child's other parent, and vice versa.

The mystery of the Most Holy Trinity is a mystery of love: "God himself is an eternal exchange of love, Father, Son and Holy Spirit, and he has destined us to share in that exchange" (CCC 221). Families naturally image the Trinity, which means we are called to love one another in our families and help our children do the same. (For guidance on how to use your divorce as a teaching opportunity regarding the Sacrament of Marriage, please see What the Church Says in chapter 12.)

Thorny Situations

Your Child Wants More Details

As your child digests the reality of your separation or divorce, she may want more detailed explanations about why it happened and the like. Some parents shut this topic down immediately by saying, "You will find out when you are older." While this response may be better than sharing inappropriate details, children will key into the *how* of what was said and may become even more curious and distracted by what they are not being told. This, of course, is a delicate balancing act. In addition, even if your child is older and has more maturity and experience regarding the intimacy of romantic relationships, it is still generally best to adhere to a "need to know" principle and keep intimate details confidential.

I heard inappropriate details from both my parents regarding the breakdown of their marriage. Even though I knew their anger was justified and drove them to make the comments, it still did me no good. Instead, the comments angered me because each parent remained my parent, someone whom I loved dearly and who was part of me. I wanted to shout back in anger, *You have no right to talk about my parent this way!* Other times, I felt completely disrespected and used, as I knew there was another side to the story that was not being reported.

If your child asks for more explanation about your specific

situation, move your conversation to the teaching level. In particular, share information that will be useful and can instill the example you want to set. For example, if your child wants to know why you and her dad are still mad at each other, you can share that forgiveness is hard for you and taking more time than you would like, but you are committed to working on it because it is what is required of a Catholic Christian.

Your Child Witnessed Domestic Violence

Seeing, hearing, or observing the aftermath of domestic violence is horrific for children. In addition, they often keep the abuse a family secret because they feel paralyzed by fear or shame. Just as it is important to talk about the divorce or separation in simple, concrete, age-appropriate ways, it will also help your child to have opportunities to discuss feelings about any domestic violence that has occurred in your home. It is certainly understandable not to want to talk about such a sensitive and upsetting matter. However, not doing so creates only more fear, isolation, and confusion for children, who likely know more about the domestic violence than their parents realize. The way to give children permission to talk about it is to raise the subject yourself, doing so with the support of a therapist and/or children's book. Otherwise, children may conclude that the topic is too shameful to explore, which prevents them from healing and achieving a greater sense of safety.

Similarly, if there is a protective order and your child's other parent is no longer permitted to see your child, explain this in simple terms. For example, "The bad news is that there has been some bad behavior and your mom/dad cannot see you right now, but the good news is that your mom/dad still loves you very much."

As with talking about reasons for the divorce or separation, do not wait to broach this topic. Refer back to the "Practical Suggestions" section of this chapter for additional guidance.

Questions for Reflection

1. Have I discussed the separation or divorce with my child? If "yes," how would I rate the job I have done from 1 to 10 (with 10 being the best)? Why? If "no," what is preventing me from having this discussion? What has been my experience in having other difficult conversations with my child?

2. What can I do to help myself improve these communications with my child? If unsure, what could help me learn how to improve in this area (i.e., journaling, talking with someone whom I trust about my difficulties and needs, etc.)?

3. Am I at peace about my separation or divorce, or do I have questions or worries? Do I need to seek counsel from my pastor or a trusted priest?

CHAPTER FOUR
Understanding Divorce Problems That May Arise and Your Child's Reaction to Them

So far, we have explored how your child is viewing the separation or divorce and how to use helping skills to draw out his concerns and affirm his feelings. Your child will continue to need you to take the lead in helping him identify and work through divorce-related problems which he may be experiencing. The problems that children may face during and following a divorce are too numerous to explore in this chapter. They may involve visitation (e.g., not feeling comfortable in the other parent's house and/or not having friends in a parent's new neighborhood; missing the parent that your child is not with; not having sufficient exclusive time when visiting a parent; doing only what the parent wants and not what the child wants; moving between houses and forgetting items); new relationships (e.g., not liking a parent's dating partner or feeling guilty about liking him or her; anger toward a stepparent who takes on a discipline role); finances (e.g., not having money for vacation and other luxuries once enjoyed, having to sell a house or leave a private school); added home responsibilities for him (e.g., helping with a younger sibling, doing more household chores, etc.); and so on. The good news is that, as extensive and challenging as these problems may be, your child can definitely learn ways to solve them with your help coaching him from the sidelines.

I want to call your attention to two problems in particular, as they have been the most common ones that children have shared with me. The first problem is parents putting their child in the middle of the divorce conflict. This can take various forms along a continuum. At one end, a parent may confide in the child inappropriately, mistakenly concluding that the honesty will be helpful to the child's emotional growth. At the other end, both parents may express outright hostility toward each other when the child is present or in earshot. In both cases, parents are unable to contain their grief sufficiently or are misinformed about their child's needs and, as a result, inadvertently create more burdens for their child.

Another common problem area results when parents fail to accept that their children do not get divorced from their divorced parents. Even when a parent is absent or a wonderful stepparent joins the family, in the child's eyes, the attachment to or longing for the biological parent remains, as that parent will always be part of the child. Divorcing parents need to accept this fact. The Catechism is clear: "A child may not be considered a piece of property, an idea to which an alleged 'right to a child' would lead. In this area, only the child possesses genuine rights: the right 'to be the fruit of the specific act of the conjugal love of his parents,' and 'the right to be respected as a person from the moment of his conception'" (CCC 2378).

When it comes to alleviating problems for your child, an essential place to start is by finding a way to communicate constructively with your child's other parent, particularly regarding matters involving your child. Some parents find email communication helpful. Others utilize a divorce mediator or family counselor. Improving communication with your ex-spouse benefits your child tremendously. It provides her with a solid emotional base that supports her exploration of the world and her interactions with others. Otherwise, your child can easily lose confidence in herself and withdraw from school and normal pursuits for her age. She may also distance herself psychologically from you in order to regain her own emotional footing. Or, as is a common tendency with girls, your child may push away her feelings and, instead, focus on being overly understanding and helpful to you and/or her other parent. That reaction can easily put your child in an enmeshed role where she tries to please by listening to problems or doing excessive chores, either of which can increase her anxiety. When parents fail to communicate constructively, the child feels like she is driving over a massive bridge with no guard rails, unsafe in moving forward. The loyalty and internal conflicts that can result for your child in these situations are explored in chapter 6.

Additional problems reported by children stem from their own personal adjustment to the divorce or separation. For example, some children are distracted because parents have not given them sufficient explanation for the divorce. Others feel they do not have permission to miss one parent without the other parent getting upset. Many complain about not having exclusive time with a parent who is dating. Older children, in particular, often worry about the emotional well-being of their parents and younger siblings.

Your child will need you to help her identify these personal problems and learn skills for communicating constructively about them. Otherwise, she will likely feel powerless or so stressed about solving them that she shuts down, which, in turn, makes the situation worse. Read on for further guidance regarding how to help your child move forward.

Practical Suggestions

1. Start with empathy, then give space.

In order for your child to identify and communicate about a divorce-related problem, he first needs to be calm enough to think about it and gain self-awareness. To help him gain calmness, you will need to communicate a nonjudgmental understanding of his perspective. Then, stop talking and give your child space to respond. This validation will likely encourage him to share more. This step will require the same skill of empathy that was addressed in the responding skills section of chapter 2 (see Practical Suggestion #4). However, since a problem-solving component is involved, you may need to give more than one empathic response so your child's needs can be more clearly identified. Here is an example:

> **Child:** "I don't want to go to Dad's this weekend. He never talks to me."
> **Empathic response:** "You don't see the point in spending time with your dad if he is not going to talk with you."

> **Child:** "Exactly. He is always on his cell phone or the computer."
> **Empathic response:** "You don't like the way your dad is treating you. It feels like he doesn't care that you are there, and that hurts."

> **Child:** "Yeah, it gets me even angrier when we go somewhere and he brings his girlfriend along."
> **Empathic response:** "I can hear how unhappy you are about your dad's new girlfriend. It sounds like you wish he would spend more time with just you alone. Am I getting that right?"

You can also show empathy by restating your child's response in different words. If you are uncomfortable with or find it difficult to communicate empathy in the way just described, simply restate what your child has told you in different words. That will let him know he has been heard and help to validate his perspective. He may likely go on to share more, which will help in clarifying the source of his problem.

Remember: You do not need to do this perfectly. After responding, just ask your child, "Am I on the right track?" or "Did I get that right?" He will likely tell you, either way, and appreciate your effort.

2. Teach your child how to calm herself down.

It is important to teach your child how to calm herself down when faced with a divorce problem, especially when you are not there. This instruction will help her with other problems she may face as well. Help her develop these skills by:

- **Teaching her to notice her own emotion(s):** Ask your child to stop and state what emotion she is experiencing when confronted with a problem. Is she angry, scared, sad, worried, frustrated, etc.? Noticing emotions will help her hit the "pause" button and avoid saying or doing something she later regrets, or that will create more problems for her.
- **Instructing her to breathe deeply:** Deep breathing helps to get more oxygen into the bloodstream and helps the child get in control of his thoughts. With preadolescents, I teach "triangle breathing": Breathe in for three counts (one side of the triangle); hold breath for three counts (second side); breathe out slowly for five counts or more (third side). The last part has a longer count to emphasize an elongated outbreath. With younger children, I teach "belly breathing" by using this analogy: Smell your fa-

vorite hot food by breathing in through your nose, then breathe out through your mouth to cool the food down so you can eat it. Or you can teach them "pizza, birthday cake," where they imagine smelling pizza, then blowing out birthday candles. Younger children can find it helpful to move a finger along the sides of the fingers of their other hand, breathing in while moving their finger up and breathing out when moving it down.

- **Encouraging the use of positive self-talk:** As a parent, you know full well how difficult it is to combat the various negative influences that our culture has on your child, in addition to the false messages that she may be telling herself. Positive self-talk is powerful ammunition in both respects, as it helps children develop a self-concept that is internally, versus externally, based. As a result, it helps them to empower themselves. You know your child best and what she needs to work on. Teach her an affirmation that would be helpful for her in whatever way she most needs it, such as: "I am capable"; "I believe in myself"; "I am smart and can figure this out"; and so on. Encourage your child to write down the affirmation and post it in her room or notebook so she can see it often. You can also surprise your child at school by putting affirmations in her lunch bag (for example, a note reminding her she is special).

Also be careful to observe your own self-talk. Hearing you speak lovingly to yourself provides your child a powerful example for doing the same.

3. Resist the urge to fix. Provide a calm anchor instead.

It is natural to rush in to try and fix your child's problem. You may want his pain to go away or, in the midst of a hectic schedule, want the issue crossed off your to-do list. If this describes you, resist the urge to take over your child's problem and solve it for him. It will require patience, energy, and self-restraint on your part, but will pay off in the long term in helping him develop the problem-solving skills he will need for other dilemmas that he will inevitably face in the future. Discipline yourself to get out of your child's way, unless the risks are too high not to step in.

Meaningful Connection Time with Your Child

Before your child can take action to solve his divorce- or separation-related problems, she needs to be in the right frame of mind emotionally and mentally. In order to get there, she needs to experience your empathy, as mentioned earlier in this chapter. Empathy will calm your child down so she can better think her problem through. Once that is accomplished, here are some steps you can take to connect with your child in a meaningful way.

1. Help your child identify a pressing problem.
You likely have an idea of what problem your child is struggling with the most as a result of your divorce or separation. However, it is important for your child to identify the problem herself. This will help her take ownership and feel she has permission to talk about the problem.

If your child is finding it difficult to identify a problem, broach the topic by discussing common problems that children experience when parents divorce, including the one you think or know is affecting your child. You can say something like, "When parents divorce or separate, many kids say they have trouble with X [including anything relevant to your child]," then give your child a chance to respond. She may share more with you. Or, if unsure whether it is safe to disclose more, she may nod, but not comment. In that case, continue your helping skills by saying something like, "I see you nodding your head. Which problem are you struggling with?"

During this discussion, young people can be quick to blame someone for the problem, either because they fear getting in trouble or because accepting responsibility is hard to do. If your child responds by blaming, calmly explain that blaming will not help solve the problem. Then, help him state it more objectively by explaining, for example, how he would describe the problem if his friend was experiencing it.

As with other divorce-related discussions, the purpose of this one is the same: to give your child permission to air her side and arm her with tools to learn, grow, and help herself.

2. Ask your child what improvement or change he would like to see.

This step can help your child more clearly identify a problem. Additionally, it helps him brainstorm solutions after he has identified a problem to work on.

Start by drawing on his imagination and asking a "miracle question." A miracle question, also referred to as a "problem is gone" question, is a goal-setting question used in Solution Focused Brief Therapy. It can be phrased this way: "Imagine that tonight, while you are sleeping, a miracle occurs. When you wake up, the problems with the separation (or divorce) are gone. What will be different for you?"

I often use miracle questions with children, and they readily engage with them. Even when a child mentions something "unrealistic," such as divorced parents getting remarried, I simply acknowledge that wish and ask, "How would that make a difference?" Asking that question once (or twice) helps the child get more in touch with what he wants or needs. The goal is to help your child give descriptions in concrete, behavioral terms, such as describing "What will your dad do differently? How will your time with him be spent differently?"

If your child is younger and does not understand what a miracle is, you can phrase the question in other ways, such as:

Magic Wand: "Suppose I had a magic wand that I could wave and make your problem disappear. When you would _____ (e.g., see your dad again, etc.), how would you notice that the wand had worked?"

Superhero: "Suppose you had powers like a superhero, how would you like to use them to handle this problem?"

Saints and Angels: "If you asked the saints and/or angels to help you as you tried to solve your problem, how would you know they had done so? What change would occur?"

Next, continue the discussion by letting your child know that miracles usually do not happen overnight, and prayers may not be answered right away or in the way we expect. Good changes can take a long time to happen. Then, ask your child, "What are some small, first steps that will let you know the miracle is starting to happen?"

Asking these questions helps your child identify and weigh options. Then, steps can be established and goals clarified. The questions also remind your child that solving problems takes time, planning, and hard work.

3. Brainstorm solutions by asking open-ended questions.
Using open-ended questions can also work when identifying solutions. You can simply ask your child, "What do you think you are going to do about this problem?" She may answer "I don't know" because she is upset or wants you to step in and solve the problem for her. If she is upset, increase your empathetic response. If she simply wants you to solve the problem for her, try to put the problem in an indirect context. For instance, you might ask, "How would you suggest helping your classmate if the problem occurred

with her?" Or "What advice would you give your friend if she was experiencing this problem?" If your child suggests something un-reasonable, simply ask, "What else could you try?"

Asking questions sends your child an important message: You expect her to assume some responsibility for fixing the prob-lem. You can still coach her from the sidelines or the passenger's seat. However, just like doing homework for school, your child needs you to step back and place her in the driver's seat so she can learn and improve this skill, and build her confidence.

4. Help your child weed out negative thoughts and beliefs.

During the problem-solving process, your child may have nega-tive thoughts and beliefs that keep him stuck, just as it happens to us as adults. If so, it is critical to help him weed them out and replace them with more accurate thoughts and beliefs.

In the 1950s, Albert Ellis developed Rational Emotional Behav-ior Therapy (REBT) based on the assumption that faulty thinking about events, rather than the events themselves, results in emotion-al difficulties. This, in turn, can lead to adverse behavioral conse-quences. Rational beliefs will help your child act constructively and achieve his goals. In contrast, irrational beliefs will cause him upset emotions and negative feelings, such as worry or anger, that make resolving problems and attaining goals difficult.

Once irrational beliefs are identified, they can be disputed and replaced with rational beliefs which, in turn, lead to more bal-anced emotions. In short, helping your child change his thinking can lead to more adaptive emotional and behavioral changes.

Referring back to the prior example in this chapter, for in-stance, suppose your ex-husband recently started dating someone and is bringing his new girlfriend along to outings with your ten-year-old daughter. If your daughter gets upset because she is not having exclusive time with her dad, she might tell herself that this situation is awful, that her dad should not be bringing his girl-friend along, and that, because he is her father, no longer loves her or regards her as important. Thus, she believes it is impossible for the situation to change.

To help your child handle the problem, you need to challenge her irrational beliefs. You could ask these questions to help her gain perspective, attain more balanced emotions, and react in more constructive ways:

- What is the proof that your dad has stopped loving you or thinks you are unimportant to him?
- Just because your dad has been bringing his girlfriend along to your outings, does that mean it will always be that way? Will you never be able to do something with just the two of you again?

Here are some other ways to help your child acquire more balanced, realistic thoughts:

- **"Half-full" Thinking:** Ask your child, "What good can come from trying to solve his problem?" Help him stay focused on the good.

  Children and adolescents often interpret their personal experiences in black or white terms. As a result, they may view problem-solving as leading to outcomes that are either all good or all bad, the best or the worst. This can encourage them to magnify or minimize their problem which, in turn, hinders them from moving forward.

  If your child focuses on the glass being "half-empty," acknowledge the risks but present them as "possible," not "probable." Then, remind him of the good parts of solving his problem that may be more likely to result.

- **"Predicting Success" Thinking:** Earlier in this chapter, we considered positive self-talk. "Predicting Success" is similar as it, too, helps your child focus positively on her abilities. With this strategy, you encourage your child to imagine herself being successful in having solved her problem, so that this "picture" is accessible in her mind.

Research shows that those who imagine success outperform those who imagine failure. Help your child visualize herself as having attained her goal.

What the Church Says

Helping your child work through her divorce problems gives you an excellent opportunity to share basic instruction regarding the doctrine of original sin. The Church teaches that we are created in the image of God, but because of Adam and Eve's disobedience to God, we have inherited a fallen, wounded nature (with the exception of Mary, the Mother of Our Lord, who was preserved by a special grace). "By our first parents' sin, the devil has acquired a certain domination over man, even though man remains free" (CCC 407). Our world is fallen, and that means sin and its problems touch everyone. In order to rise above those problems and avoid sinning in the future, we need to draw on a power greater than our own: God's power. We access God's power by following Jesus, praying, and receiving the sacraments, especially the Eucharist and confession. We can also call on the graces of our baptism and confirmation to strengthen us in difficult moments.

Thorny Situation

Your Child Is Trying to Solve Adult Problems

In trying to alleviate their own frustration and worry and to gain control, children may set out to solve adult problems that are not their responsibility. Many of these problems stem from "gaps" created in the family and in the personal lives of parents. Children can easily be drawn to try to fill in these gaps. For example, a child may attempt to solve a parent's loneliness by serving as a confidant. Or an older child may try to discipline a younger sibling, or assume the majority of household tasks. Children need to sense that their parents are okay in order to feel free to resume normal pursuits for their age.

As a child, I often assumed the role of emotional caretaker with both my parents. They needed adult support, but did not avail themselves of counseling or peer support groups. So I stepped in to take responsibility for fulfilling their needs. I wanted to please my parents; however, more importantly, I needed them to be okay emotionally. This response put my own grief work on hold. That grief bubbled to the surface later when I entered my first serious dating relationship. It also fostered unhealthy ways of relating to my other family members, as I enabled them to their detriment and my own. In short, I was not encouraged to develop healthy personal boundaries.

You have likely heard of boundaries before. They serve as a dividing line or limit between our personal space and that of another. They also serve an important spiritual purpose in helping us stay focused on using our time, energy, and resources for doing God's will for us. As such, they help us nurture and protect our souls.

When working with preadolescents, I describe this concept by using the analogy of cleaning their room. They are responsible for cleaning it (or part of it if they share their room with a sibling). However, they are not responsible for cleaning their parent's room. Similarly, they are not responsible for giving a parent advice, staying home to keep a parent company, being a parent's confidant, delivering messages between parents, and so on. Preadolescents typically grasp this concept on some level. I once worked with a ten-year-old whose parents were battling over how his cell phone would be used for communications among the adults, including the father's girlfriend. The boy rightly interpreted that this was his mom's problem with his dad, not his problem. However, he told me he did not want to assert himself with his mom as he sensed her need for him to listen. He responded by putting her needs first, even though he said the listening made him sad.

A preadolescent child will be more aware than a younger child of his own vulnerabilities to realities such as illness, injury, and death and, in turn, your vulnerabilities in this regard also. The stress that causes for him if you are having personal or emotional difficulties can encourage him to try and "clean up your room." Do not allow him to do this. Instead, help him learn to recognize when a task is not his responsibility, and teach him to set boundaries for himself and others so he can establish healthy relationships with you, your ex, other family members, and friends. This will lay a critical foundation for him in his other relationships as well.

Questions for Reflection

1. Have I talked to my child about my problems with my ex-spouse or other divorce-related problems? If so, are there other people in my life I can process my feelings with so I can set appropriate boundaries with my child?

2. Have I been respectful of my child's attachment to his other biological parent? What difficulties am I having in this regard?

3. What other problems might my child be having as a result of my separation or divorce? What has been my response to those difficulties?

4. How can I more fully help my child in taking ownership of his divorce problems as a disciple? What can I do (or do more of) to challenge him to grow in holiness in this way?

CHAPTER FIVE
Your Role in the Solution and How to Take Constructive Action

In the previous chapter, we addressed how many divorce-related problems for children stem from poor parental communications, unhealthy boundaries, and failures of a parent to respect the child's relationship with or attachment to her other biological parent. We also addressed how to help your child define other divorce-related problems and brainstorm solutions. In this chapter, we will explore how to help your child evaluate those solutions.

After my parents divorced, I took it upon myself to protect and heal my parents' emotional well-being. This was very unhealthy. For my mother, I would play the piano in the evenings, hoping the songs would soothe her. I also did as many chores as possible so she would have less to do. However, nothing lifted my mother's spirits more than when I received good grades in school. It was the one thing that always made her happy, and it made me feel more in control of creating something good amid the family damage around me. So I clung to my academic pursuits daily like food and water. I thought it was my way of ensuring my mother's emotional survival and keeping whatever family I had intact. The accomplishments also made me feel as if I could earn my father's attention. Here, too, I kept raising the bar higher for myself, thinking that as soon as I accomplished and proved myself worthy enough, then my father would notice me.

As a preadolescent and adolescent, I was unaware that my "addiction" to achievement was an unhealthy way to try and solve my problem, which was beyond my control. I also wasn't meeting with a counselor or another adult who could guide me in healthier directions. As a young person, I was unaware of how my solutions were harming my personal development and, most importantly, preventing me from learning who I was and God's plan for my life.

Like other topics presented in this book, your child will need your help and support here, too. Read on to learn how to help her take appropriate ownership of her divorce-related problems.

Practical Suggestions

1. Praise your child's effort.
As your child applies himself to solving problems, give positive recognition of his effort. This is particularly important when he feels discouraged, frustrated, or wants to give up. It can be a simple recognition such as, "Even though you were scared to talk with your father, you gave it a try. That took a lot of courage." Point out your child's strengths and what he does well, in the midst of any weaknesses, as this will help in building his self-confidence and encourage his persistence.

2. Encourage your child to take reasonable risks.
Praise your child also when she tries something new to solve her problem. Additionally, reassure her that making mistakes

is part of the process and, often, the best learning tool of all. This will promote her resilience and recognize her initiative as well as her success.

3. Accept your role as coach, not "fixer."
It can be difficult to hold back and allow your child to struggle when solving problems. However, unless the problem involves a safety issue, let him master the struggle and work toward finding his own solutions instead of stepping in to fix the situation for him. Otherwise, you will shortchange him of an important opportunity to grow in self-confidence and independence, which, in turn, will help him tackle other problems more successfully in the future.

4. Let your child experience unpleasant feelings in this process.
Frustration, disappointment, anger, and other unpleasant feelings arise for all of us in the course of solving problems, especially those involving family relationships. Respond in a balanced way when your child expresses these negative feelings. Do not attempt to change or mitigate them. Instead, affirm the feelings and convey understanding.

For example, you can say something like, "Yes, trying to communicate better can be frustrating. It might take a couple times to express yourself accurately." You could then offer to help by adding, "How about we try a role-play so you can practice what you'd like to say to your mother?" Or, you could express your confidence in your child's abilities by saying something like, "I am confident that you have the ability to work through this problem and solve it, like you have done before."

Other statements that affirm feelings and convey understanding:

- "It sounds like this situation has really been upsetting you."

- "I can hear how challenging this problem is."
- "You sound overwhelmed and discouraged about being able to solve this problem."

Supportive, nonenabling responses convey to your child that she can learn to cope with difficult feelings and that you have confidence in her ability to handle them. It also reminds her that problem-solving often involves an ongoing process rather than a quick fix.

Meaningful Connection Time with Your Child

1. Ask questions that reflect the values and principles you want your child to adopt.
In my work at Catholic schools, one phrase that students are repeatedly reminded of is "Be respectful, be responsible, be kind because Christ matters." This is an excellent rule to use when helping children evaluate what could happen if they use a specific divorce solution, whether it involves a parent or classmate. In particular, help your child consider possible negative and positive consequences by asking her questions such as:

- Are you communicating honestly and clearly?
- Does the solution reflect how you would like to be treated?
- Is the solution likely to hurt anyone's feelings?
- What effect might your solution have on your relationship with the other person?
- Does your solution reflect what Jesus would do? Does it respect the dignity of the other person?

2. Help your child "drill down" and choose the best solution.
Here it is important to point out to your child that the first solution he tries may not be the best one, and that is okay and

happens to everyone. Often, we learn very important things in the course of solving problems and making mistakes that help us pick an even better solution. If your child's first solution does not work, ask him what he learned and help him choose another one.

Here is an example of how I helped a student evaluate her solution:

- **Define the problem:** "My classmates found out my parents are getting divorced. They are asking me a lot of questions about it, and it is getting me upset."

- **Generate solutions:**
  1. Ignore them and walk away.
  2. Go to a different school.
  3. Answer their questions.
  4. Tell them in a respectful way that it is private, and you don't want to talk about it.

- **Evaluate the solutions:**
  1. That would be disrespectful.
  2. I like my school and do not want to leave.
  3. That would make me uncomfortable. Plus, I don't want to talk about the divorce when I'm at school.
  4. It would let them know what I want without hurting their feelings.

- **Choose a solution, practice it, then evaluate the results.**

The student chose solution #4. We discussed how the divorce was her private, family business. That did not mean she had to keep it a secret, but that she did not have to give details about it to anyone. We role-played the situation, and various statements that she could use ("It is private, and I don't want to talk about it." "It is difficult, but we're going to be okay.") I checked in with her a few days later. The student told me the questions had stopped, and she was no longer stressed about her peers.

3. For more difficult conflicts, especially as your child gets older, teach him a conflict resolution strategy, such as one of the following:

- Wait until both parties are calm enough to talk.
- Hurt/upset person starts by using an "I-statement." While I-statements can take many forms, it is helpful to give your child a basic formula for understanding the main parts involved:

  "I feel _____ (name the feeling) when you _____ (explain the action) because _____ (note the reason behind the feeling)." "I want (or do not want) _____ _____ (propose a solution)."

  "You-statements," in contrast, are aggressive, attacking responses. They do not work when solving problems because they assign blame and put the other person on the defensive. As a result, You-statements can escalate a conflict (see example below). Explain this to your child, then invite him to practice I-statements so he gets accustomed to the feeling of being assertive and can develop the skill before needing to use it.

  Example: Your child's father is an hour late in picking him up. Your child tried calling all his phone numbers, but he did not answer any of them.

  I-Message: "Dad, I am so relieved to see you! I was so worried this past hour because I thought maybe you got in an accident. If you are running late again, could you please call and let me know?"

You-Message: "Dad, why didn't you call to let me know you were running late? You really got me worried."

- Other person states his/her understanding of what was said.

For example, "So, what you are saying is ... ?" The other person can then ask open-ended questions, if needed.

- Other person states his/her point of view (using an I-statement).
- First person states his/her understanding of what the other person said.
- Process continues until both persons feel they have been heard.
- They brainstorm possible solutions.
- They choose a solution to try.
- They make a plan.
- They end by saying something nice to one another.
- For example, "I'm glad we worked things out," "I'm sorry," and "Thanks for discussing this with me."

4. Teach conversational rules.

Like any other skill, verbal communication skills can improve significantly with basic rules, instruction, and practice. Which rules are difficult for your child to adhere to? Consider the following:

- Focus on one problem at a time (rather than trying to focus on everything that he is upset about).
- Pick a good time to talk.

- Show you are listening by small verbal responses (e.g., "Uh-huh," "I understand," etc.).
- Use nonverbal responses to show listening (e.g., making eye contact, nodding, smiling, etc.).
- Take turns talking.
- Give your full attention by minimizing distractions (e.g., turn off the TV, iPad, etc.).
- Answer and ask questions.
- Tell the truth.
- Accept responsibility for your feelings.

What the Church Says

Listen Like Jesus Did

The most perplexing, heart-wrenching problem I had regarding my parents' divorce was understanding and accepting why my father was not more involved in my life. This took me many years to resolve. As a child and adolescent, I tried to solve this problem by overachieving, believing I could earn my father's attention like I had earned good grades in school. But it did not work. As a young adult, I sometimes demanded answers from my father like someone seeking justice for wrongs done to her. But that only pushed him away.

It was only when I listened to my father's side that God gave me answers. This listening required me to set my needs to the side so I could learn more about who my father was. It was then that I realized his personal struggles and weaknesses and, essentially, that he was unable to give me what I needed. This was a difficult truth to accept and my greatest cross from my parents' divorce. However, it led me to peace and, eventually, gave me the emotionally close relationship with my father that I had longed for my entire life. It was not in the way I had hoped for, but in the way God intended. I was unable to solve my problem and reach this milestone, however, until I listened to and understood my father's side.

We know from the Gospels that Jesus asked lots of questions. He listened, was present, and uncovered the truth. Teach your child to do the same. Encourage him to ask questions so he can understand the perspective of the person with whom he has a problem. He may find that he has been viewing a situation incorrectly or that he is contributing to a problem without realizing it. He may also learn that the other person has the same concerns and wants to solve the problem also. The solution may not be the one that your child is hoping for; however, by listening, he will be able to find a solution that leads to truth and peace.

Solutions must also respect the dignity of all persons involved. Catholic teaching calls us to respect the inherent dignity of others. Every person has dignity because every person is created in the image and likeness of God (CCC 1700). As a result, every person is worthy of respect and has a right to life consistent with that dignity. Remind your child of this important tenet and ask him to reflect on whether his solution respects the other person's dignity as well as his own.

Rely on the Holy Spirit

When solving problems, it is critical to encourage your child to draw on the strength and direction of the Holy Spirit, especially as provided through the sacraments. Remind her that she received sanctifying grace through her baptism, giving her the power to act through the gifts of the Holy Spirit (CCC 1266). These seven gifts are: wisdom, understanding, counsel (right judgment), fortitude (courage), knowledge, piety (reverence), and fear of the Lord (wonder and awe).

Additionally, stress to your child the importance of the Eucharist in uniting her with Jesus and increasing his grace within her. If your child has also received the Sacrament of Confirmation, explain that it deepens baptismal grace and increases the gifts of the Holy Spirit (CCC 1303). Encourage her to call on those graces and gifts in doing what God asks of her.

Emphasize to your child that when she cooperates with the Holy Spirit, uses her gifts, and receives the sacraments, good things become more present in her life. Her relationship with God can then become like a seed that grows and bears fruit. Saint Paul wrote that "the fruit of the Spirit is love, joy, peace, patience, kindness, generosity, faithfulness, gentleness, and self-control" (Gal 5:22–23). Explain this does not mean that God is like a vending machine, as God sometimes says "no," which can result in some suffering for us. What it does mean, however, is that God knows what is best for us, has a perfect plan, and will surprise us with many good things if we cooperate with grace.

Ask your child:

- What gifts of the Holy Spirit can help her in solving her divorce-related problems?
- What does she need to strengthen in herself when solving these problems so she may show love more fully?
- What fruits of the Holy Spirit are developing within her as she cooperates with him in working through these problems?'

Thorny Situation

Your Child Is Not Accepting Responsibility

Not only do children experience new problems when parents divorce or separate, but those problems are often ones that they feel unable or unprepared to handle. This is why a good place to start is with responding skills (see chapter 2, Practical Suggestion #4 on page 41) and the suggestions noted earlier in this chapter. Those interventions can help your child in reducing his stress and empower him with a sense of control. Another reason why your child may not be accepting responsibility for solving his divorce-related problems is because he may lack what psychologists call self-efficacy or a belief in his ability to succeed. Perhaps your child has already attempted to solve his problem (or a similar problem), and things did not turn out well. His self-esteem may have diminished to the point where he views a mistake or failure as who he is rather than what he did. If this describes your child, reaffirm his effort so he may be encouraged to persevere and develop self-respect. By the same token, it is also important to clarify for your child what is his responsibility and not allow him to blame others or make excuses for himself. Explain that if he avoids taking responsibility, he is breaking trust with others.

Questions for Reflection

1. What example am I setting for my child regarding problem solving? What do I do well? What do I do not so well?

2. What gifts of the Holy Spirit would I like to strengthen in myself when solving difficulties regarding my divorce or separation?

3. What gifts is the Holy Spirit calling me to use in order to help my child solve his or her divorce-related problems?

CHAPTER SIX
How Being Put in the Middle Harms Children Psychologically and How to Avoid It

My father put me in the middle of his conflict with my mother without me fully realizing it. From my earliest memory, I had been his confidant as he told me details about his childhood. It made me uncomfortable to hear these details, and I did not understand why he was telling me about them. Nevertheless, I listened because I sensed my father needed me to, and because, more than anything, I wanted to have a close relationship with him. As I became a teenager, he began to share his regrets in having moved so far away and his experiences when dating my mom and, later, being married to her. These details were often disparaging. It felt wrong to have my mother portrayed in such a negative light. After all, this was my mother he was talking about! And he surely would not want someone talking badly about his mother. I felt manipulated and sensed that it was wrong for me to be treated this way. I also knew there were two sides to the story regarding my parents' marital problems.

Still, I listened. I was always interested in learning the truth, anything that would shed light on who my parents were and why their marriage failed. As a child, the divorce always felt like a "big, bad thing," even though it afforded much needed relief from my parents' frequent fighting. I had to find a way to deal with that "big, bad thing," much like someone needs to find a way to handle a major illness beyond their control. For me, that meant learning as much as possible so I could apply that knowledge in my own life, turning a negative into a positive.

Because my parents lived far away from each other for the majority of their separation and divorce, I was spared being put directly in the middle as often as can happen with children who spend regular time in each home. However, the destructive conflict I witnessed between my parents when they lived together left a permanent mark that caused me appreciable confusion and anguish later as a young adult in my dating relationships. I never got used to that conflict. Instead, like treating your body badly, the damage had a cumulative effect.

What about you and your ex-spouse? Is your child witnessing destructive fighting between the two of you? Are you putting your child in the middle as a result of these conflicts? Read on to learn common ways this can happen. If any describe your situation, be aware that destructive conflict strategies, intense arguments, and unresolved emotional tension undermine children's emotional security, while constructive strategies, well-resolved conflicts, and restoration of good feelings result in largely adaptive coping skills.[10] Many divorcing parents, understandably, need help to contain and minimize their conflict. If this is your

---

10. K. McCoy, E. M. Cummings, and P. T. Davies, "Constructive and destructive marital conflict, emotional security and children's prosocial behavior," J. Child Psychol. Psychiatry, 50, no. 3 (March 2009): 270–279.

situation, consider family therapy and/or divorce mediation. It can be a very beneficial investment.

Ways of Putting Kids in the Middle

Going through a divorce or separation can steal the best from any parent, as you likely know full well. You can easily become exasperated and put your child in the cross fire without realizing it. Or perhaps you do realize it but assume such actions are not harmful for your child. If so, I encourage you to stop and consider these incidents from your child's point of view. When children are put in the middle, no matter how inadvertently, they feel pressured to take sides, which means they must be disloyal to a parent. They may also feel burdened by an inappropriate expectation to serve as a confidant and look after a parent's emotional and psychological well-being.

Here are common ways this can happen.

Projecting parental distress onto your child

Even if you initiated the divorce, you will likely experience a grief reaction because of the breakup of your marriage. After all, you did not get married expecting or hoping to get divorced. Your child's reactions can easily aggravate these wounds, encouraging you to project your distress onto him or her. After my parents' divorce, whenever I expressed disappointment about something my dad did or did not do, my mother would get very upset and respond either by sharing his past transgressions or giving me harsh advice. Her intentions were good. She was convinced my father would only hurt me like he had hurt her, and she wanted to protect me. However, her unresolved grief dominated these sharings and led her to share inappropriate details with me. Intuitively, I understood that and discredited her conclusions and advice as a result. I also was not ready to digest the reality she was forcing upon me. Instead, I needed someone to affirm and empathize with my grief. Because my mother was unable to do that at the time, her response ended up being more harmful than helpful. I responded by digging in my heels, determined to prove her wrong.

Another way that distress can be projected onto a child is when parents regularly overshare what is going on in their personal lives, in the absence of any trigger from their child. Psychologists refer to this as "parentification," and it happens when a parent relies on the child for emotional support, as a confidant or advisor. The child, in turn, feels responsible for looking after the parent's emotional and psychological well-being and often overlooks their own normal developmental pursuits in the process. According to Jankowski et al. (2011), early parentification puts children at increased risk for anxiety, depression, eating disorders, and substance misuse as adults.[11]

Vilifying the other parent

Vilifying is similar to projecting parental distress, but it is driven by anger and, often, a need to ensure a child's loyalty. On a deeper level, as with my dad, it can also be a parent's way of trying to assuage guilt, especially if he was the one who initiated the divorce. Vilifiers take advantage of opportunities to demean the other parent. This can include sharing adult information that is highly inappropriate for the child to hear (details about legal difficulties, intimate details about past indiscretions, psychological difficulties, etc.).

I have worked with many divorcing parents who do this in the school setting, whether during a parent meeting or in the school lobby for all passersby to hear. Sometimes, they are simply venting. Other times, they are seeking to rally school personnel to take their side. Whatever the motive, it not only reflects

---

11. P. J. Jankowski, L. M. Hooper, S. J. Sandage, and N. J. Hannah, "Parentification and mental health symptoms: mediator effects of perceived unfairness and differentiation of self," Journal of Family Therapy 35, no. 1 (2011): 45.

badly on them, but also calls attention to them as a major source of their child's problem, especially when the child has behavioral difficulties.

Researchers state that boys are more likely to hear hostile or derogatory comments about their father from their mother. This can weaken the father/son bond and cause boys to suffer more negative consequences than girls. Richard A. Warshak, a psychologist and author of *Custody Revolution*, says, "A mother's negative opinion of her former spouse, if conveyed to her son, can do more harm to his gender identification and his self-esteem than can the lack of contact with his father. Rarely does a boy hold a negative opinion of his father without holding the same opinion of himself."[12]

Investigating your child
Investigating is when a parent asks the child for information about the other parent. It can be similar to vilifying if the parent is looking to collect ammunition to use against the other parent. Or the questioning parent may just be curious about the other parent's activities and ask the child to report on them. Whatever the intention, investigating can put appreciable stress on your child because it places her in a "no-win" situation. On one hand, your child may want to obey or please you; however, this comes at the price of showing disloyalty or gossiping about her other parent. It certainly is acceptable to ask questions to ensure your child's safety, but meddling is inappropriate, disrespects your child, and will cause her additional stress.

Overindulging your child
Parents who exhibit this behavior are commonly referred to as "Disneyland Parents," who placate their children with gifts or lax rules. This overindulgence can be an attempt to win a child's af-

---

12. R. A. Warshak, PhD. *Custody Revolution: Father Custody and the Motherhood Mystique* (New York: Simon & Schuster, 1992), 163.

fections, or it can be a way of making life more difficult for the other parent who cannot afford expensive gifts and outings, or who insists on disciplining the child regarding things like homework, chores, and earlier bedtimes. This overindulgence can also occur with a girlfriend or boyfriend who steps in and tries to eradicate the other parent's role by attending school events, baking special treats, and the like.

Asking your child to deliver messages

Perhaps you have asked your child to deliver a message for you, because it is so much easier than communicating directly with your ex-spouse. From your point of view, it may seem harmless. However, it can easily cause a number of problems for everyone, including you. First, the other parent may be upset by the message and your child has to experience the unpleasant fallout and be left feeling responsible for it. Not only is that unfair, but it also puts your child directly in the combat zone, which is psychologically damaging for him. Second, your child may not remember the message accurately. Or he may not mention it at all in an attempt to avoid a potential conflict. In both cases, communication fails. No matter how insignificant a message might seem, get in the routine of delivering it yourself. The more you and your ex-spouse can learn to be good "business partners," the better it will be for everyone, especially your child.

The Impact of Witnessing Destructive Conflict

Research shows that conflict between parents is detrimental to children when it is destructive, frequent, and intense. Many parents do not realize the extent to which their child is harmed by it. According to Cummings and Davies in *Children and Marital Conflict*, parental conflict disrupts children's emotional functioning because emotional security is a product of past experiences with marital conflict and a primary influence on future responding. They state that conflict disrupts three areas for children:

1. First, conflict triggers an emotional reaction (such as sadness, fear, or anger). The nature and depth of emotional arousal, along with how well the child can manage these emotions, is one factor that affects the impact on the child's adjustment.
2. A second factor is how children perceive family relationships as a result of the conflict. For example, does the conflict cause the child to feel anxious about the potential for conflict between himself and you or his other parent, or his siblings? As a result, the child may perceive that family relationships are insecure.
3. A third factor focuses on how the child manages his exposure to parental conflict. Does he intervene to try and stop it, or does he keep out of the way?

The first factor created the most disruption for me. When I reflect back, I do not remember much about my childhood, except for those occasions when my parents fought destructively. I can still hear the dishes and pans clanking in the kitchen sink, the slamming of cupboards, and the yelling. I also remember the tension when my older brother, Marc, and I sat together upstairs, worrying and wondering when the fighting would end. We remained trapped during those years, too afraid and too young to do anything about it.

The tension would start as soon as my father arrived home, and it persisted even when my parents were not yelling. During dinner, I sat silently, careful not to make any noise that might ignite an eruption from or between my parents. In the evenings the tension sometimes subsided, and each of us would retreat to our bedrooms, while my dad either read in his study or went into the family room to play music with the door shut. But the tension never went away completely. We knew it was just a matter of time before the fighting would erupt again. One message was consistent: My parents were having major problems in their marriage that were only getting worse. And I was powerless to help, except to try and be strong for my mother whenever she turned to me for support.

Twelve years after my father left home, the debris from my parents' fighting erupted in my first serious dating relationship. When major conflicts arose with my boyfriend, I was thrown back in time and relived the moments when my parents fought. I could not see through the clouds of dust that were being kicked up, and I overreacted. Emotionally, I returned to the place I occupied when my parents fought. The difference, though, was that I was old enough to leave and assert my power, which I did by giving ultimatums and threats to end the relationship. Something controlled me in those moments, but I had no idea what it was. All I knew was that I was not going to be "defeated" like I had seen my mother defeated. I fought back, yet I did so as if in her skin.

As a young adult, I was experiencing what research psychologist Judith Wallerstein and science writer Sandra Blakeslee named the "sleeper effect" in their book *Second Chances: Men, Women and Children a Decade After Divorce*. Although I had already begun grieving the loss of my father, my reaction to the breakdown of my parents' marriage had been delayed. As the fears and anxieties in my dating relationship grew, they dislodged similar fears and anxieties I had experienced when my parents fought. Like a volcano, I erupted. Wallerstein and Blakeslee say the sleeper effect typically affects women in young adulthood when they face issues of commitment and love. I share this with you because it illustrates how pervasive destructive parental conflict can be, possibly impacting your child for years if not over a decade. I believe the sleeper effect accounts for much of the reason why women from divorced families experience a higher divorce rate than men from divorced families, as well as when compared to women from intact families.

Practical Suggestions

You may have tried a myriad of positive ways to communicate with your ex-spouse: email, text, family counseling, mediation, or even trying to work with your ex's current partner. Perhaps, despite your efforts to take the high road, you still encounter vitriol from your child's other parent, with no improvement in communication between you. It may seem like a no-win situation. Yet no matter how uncooperative your child's other parent may be with you, you can still model important attitudes regarding conflict resolution for your child's benefit.

1. Try to express empathy or kindness when commenting on your conflict with the other parent.
If your child asks or comments about your conflict with his other parent, try to shelve anger and show an understanding attitude. For example, say something like, "The separation has been difficult for your father, as well as us. He is having difficulty managing his anger right now. Hopefully, we will be able to communicate better in the future." This attitude, while very difficult to embrace, does your child more good than assigning blame. The more you can treat the other parent as being on the same team as you (which remains true no matter what), the better for everyone.

2. Refrain from destructive criticism of your child.
When your child makes a mistake, try not to react in exasperation, anger, or disapproval. Instead, try to calmly discuss how to do something better the next time. By experiencing a kind response from you, your child will be more likely to show kindness to others.

3. Teach negotiation and compromise when solving conflicts at home.
You can practice conflict resolution strategies in low-risk situ-

ations at home. Perhaps your child wants to go somewhere different for vacation or objects to eating a certain meal. While you might be willing to compromise, consider instead using the conflict resolution strategy noted in chapter 5 (Meaningful Connection Time with Your Child, #3 on page 82). This strategy models responsible communication and will help your child learn to regulate his emotions, which he can later draw on when solving other conflicts.

Meaningful Connection Time with Your Child

Because you are the parent and she is the child, there is a natural power differential in your relationship with your child. As a result, she may be unwilling to share with you her distress about being put in the middle between you and her other parent. Children have often expressed to me their fear of a parent getting mad at them if they speak up about these problems. Others are reluctant to admit them because they know their parent is struggling emotionally and they do not want to add to the distress. Here are some ways you can connect with your child, address any wounds that may have been caused, and avoid causing further hurt in the future.

1. Start by apologizing.
Have you bad-mouthed your child's other parent in front of her? Told her inappropriate details? Asked her to report on what her other parent said or did? Had her deliver messages for you? Reflect honestly on this possibility and, if you have put your child in the middle, apologize for what you have done. Not only is your child owed an apology, but it may encourage her to share her side of the situation.

2. Ask your child about behaviors that concern you.
Even if your child does not verbally express concern about be-

ing put in the middle, his behavior may signal that he is experiencing distress. For example, a child who has consistently been obedient at home may start arguing about chores or rules. Or he may act very differently than before with a parent, or lose interest in extracurricular activities and schoolwork. At the other extreme, a child may become focused on pleasing and meeting another's needs on an ongoing basis, at the expense of his own. He may lack understanding and awareness of what he is responsible for and what he is not, because he has not established clear boundaries.

Being put in the middle takes a tremendous emotional toll on children because they love both their parents. Many children of divorce feel a loyalty conflict between their parents to begin with. That conflict intensifies when they hear bad-mouthing, are asked to be a messenger or spy, or sense that one or both of their parents is having difficulty caring for themselves. They feel tremendous guilt and anxiety because they are repeatedly being asked to be disloyal to one parent or the other, or to take on a caretaking role.

Being put in the middle can also intensify the anger that a child may already feel about the divorce. Since that anger is at odds with the child's love for his parents, it creates a major internal conflict for the child, which he may try to resolve by arguing with a parent or withdrawing. These behaviors can be the child's way of getting even with parents and gaining control. Such internal conflicts are particularly worrisome in adolescents given their capacity to engage in more destructive behaviors.

3. Honestly assess if you (and/or your child) need outside support with this problem.

Parents have shared with me that the divorce process was more difficult than they had anticipated, and, as a result, they succumbed to unhealthy ways of coping. For example, one parent was so afraid of losing her child to an ex-spouse's new partner that she told her child disparaging details about the other parent, shared legal communications, and the like. The child, wanting to protect her parent emotionally, tried to meet her needs by listening and emotionally supporting her parent, even though it made her uncomfortable and sad. Situations such as this nurture codependency. They are not responsible ways to care for others or oneself. It also gets us off the path of becoming the person God meant for us to be. Honestly ask yourself, and/or someone who knows you well and will be honest with you, whether you are coping responsibly with the divorce. If not, enlist professional help. It can make a major positive difference for you and your child.

What the Church Says

The fourth commandment tells us to "Honor your father and your mother, so that your days may be long in the land which the Lord your God is giving you" (Ex 20:12; Dt 5:16). This commandment tells us that children are required to show respect toward parents and not hold on to ill feelings because of their mistakes, limitations, and/or failures. Even if love and guidance are lacking, children should appreciate their parents for giving them the gift of life. This commandment, therefore, serves to uphold the goodness of the family as well. When children witness one parent disrespecting the other by vilifying, revealing derogatory information, and the like, they see this commandment rejected and can easily adopt the attitude that their parent (or both parents) is not worthy of their respect, either. During one of my divorce groups for children, a fourth-grader specifically told me that the fourth commandment did not apply to her because her parents were divorced. Divorcing parents have shared similar sentiments, telling me they were glad their child "knew the facts" that were causing him to shun his other parent. Similarly, divorced mothers with whom I have worked have condoned their children's refusal to write their father's last name on school papers. While the anger in these situations may be understandable, it fosters a no-win situation when used as a weapon. It only thwarts the child's forgiveness of a parent (or both parents), which stifles his personal healing and will cause him to carry this baggage into his future relationships. It could even alienate him from God and the Church in the process.

The Catechism states that failure to observe the fourth commandment "brings great harm to communities and to individuals." On the other hand, following this commandment provides "along with spiritual fruits, temporal fruits of peace and prosperity" (CCC 2200). Additionally, "God has willed that, after him, we should honor our parents to whom we owe life. ... We are obliged to honor and respect all those whom God, for our good, has vested with his authority" (CCC 2197). While this commandment can be challenging to uphold, it leads to lasting peace. Remember that God's grace is always there to help you achieve it.

Thorny Situation

Other Parent Putting Your Child in the Middle

If your child's other parent is bad-mouthing you, sharing inappropriate divorce details with your child, or doing other things that put her in the middle, it is likely infuriating and pushing other vulnerable buttons for you. Understandably, the urge may be to hurl an accusation back or share other inappropriate details to even the score. You may even feel justified in doing so. While it can be very difficult to step back from this fight and maintain composure, you must do so in order to respond in a healthy way for your child. Not doing so will only add to her harm. Using the responding skills section of chapter 2 (see Practical Suggestion #4 on page 41) will help you. For example, "You sound really mad/confused/afraid about that." Or, "I'm sorry you were shown that information. Legal disputes are adult matters." As with other divorce conversations, these ones need to be about your child's feelings, not yours.

The benefit of succeeding with this challenging task is huge. It allows you to tend to your child's fear, anger, confusion, and so on so he can free himself from the war zone and find his own space for healing. It also reinforces emotional safety for him, which is critically important. As a result of experiencing this safety, your child will be encouraged to share more, versus less, with you in the future.

Questions for Reflection

1. In what ways have I put my child in the middle of my conflict with my ex-spouse? How has the distress from this situation manifested in my child?

2. Are there emotions that I am expressing too frequently or too openly with my child (anger, sadness, guilt, etc.)? In what ways might my child feel put in the middle as a result? What can I do to manage my emotions better and model appropriate emotional expression?

3. If my own parents are still alive, does my child witness me abiding by the fourth commandment with them? Do I speak to my parents with respect and patience, spend time with them, and offer them help?

CHAPTER SEVEN
The Effect Your Anger Has on Your Child and What to Do about It

As mentioned earlier, my parents fought destructively for years before they separated. They were grappling with significant stressors at the time, and they did not get professional help for them. Instead, they let anger take over, and it contributed, eventually, to the destruction of their marriage. The anger also created an explosion throughout our home. That explosive material stayed with me for over a decade, erupting when I entered my first serious dating relationship as a young adult. After that relationship ended, I realized I had reacted to the anger I had witnessed between my parents as a child that had been powerless to do anything about.

Anger is a common emotion experienced by divorcing parents. It is also one of the most (if not *the* most) destructive emotions for children to witness. In a study of naturally occurring episodes of anger existing between parents, children exposed to more frequent marital conflict reacted more intensely when exposed to a later episode of parental conflict than did children who had experienced less frequent conflict.[13] Additionally, children who had witnessed two angry confrontations between adult experimenters in a laboratory behaved more aggressively toward a peer than those who had observed only one such conflict.[14] This suggests that witnessing angry interactions between parents may lead children to perceive aggression as acceptable.

I worked with an eight-year-old who expressed his anger over his parents' separation through misbehavior in the classroom. He would openly tell his classmates how much he hated his father and, despite being very intelligent, often refused to do classwork. When the teacher took disciplinary action, he reacted angrily. He said her assignments were dumb, refused to talk to her, became highly distracting in class, and threw his papers on the floor. During school meetings, the mother's anger toward the father was palpable and openly expressed. The following school year, as the parents entered mediation and co-parenting education classes, their anger subsided, and the boy became less disobedient and disruptive in the classroom.

Judith Wallerstein found that anger in children of divorce typically lessens in intensity over time. Some children, however, hold onto anger by adopting a highly critical view of their parents' immoral behavior during the marriage.[15] At the ten-year mark post-breakup, the majority of young people in Wallerstein's study concluded that their parents were ill-suited to each other. Many of those who remained angry continued

13. E. M. Cummings, C. Zahn-Waxler, and M. Radke-Yarrow, "Young children's responses to expressions of anger and affection by others in the family," Child Development 52, no. 4 (1981): 1274–1281.
14. E. M. Cummings, R. J. Iannotti, and C. Zahn-Waxler, "Influence of conflict between adults on the emotions and aggression of young children," Developmental Psychology 21, no. 3 (1985): 495–507.
15. J. S. Wallerstein, "Children of Divorce: Preliminary Report of a Ten-Year Follow-up of Older Children and Adolescents," Journal of the American Academy of Child Psychiatry 24, no. 5 (1985): 545–553.

to criticize their parents for past irresponsible or immoral conduct; many were also angry that their parents had not corrected their problems prior to having children.

Practical Suggestions

According to Judith Wallerstein and Sandra Blakeslee, authors of *Second Chances: Men, Women and Children a Decade After Divorce*, "One-half of the women and one-third of the men are still intensely angry at their former spouses" after ten years. Such anger, they write, "has become an ongoing, and sometimes dominant, presence in their children's lives as well."[16] Thus, as with many facets of helping your children through divorce, the essential starting point is to help yourself so you can better support your child. Here are some ways you can handle your own anger constructively, and then help your child face his or her anger in healthy ways.

1. Be aware of your anger and what you are modeling for your child regarding it.
Anger can be difficult for any of us to control. You may be appalled at something your ex-spouse says or does and want to get even or put them in their place, especially when the matter involves something as important as your child. Past hurts in your marriage can easily be kicked up and intensify present anger as well. It can be tempting to give in to anger because it makes us feel more powerful in the short-term. As a result, we can start to rely on our anger to avoid feelings that are more difficult, such as sadness, fear, or guilt.

The urge to engage and fight back, whether at an ex-spouse or by venting in your child's presence, can be overwhelming. Be-

16. J. S. Wallerstein and S. Blakeslee, *Second Chances: Men, Women and Children a Decade After Divorce* (Independently Published, 2018), 31.

fore you do, though, stop and ask yourself:

- Is this a fight worth picking? Is this issue really that important to "win"?
- What would be the consequence for you/your child if you "lost"? Is (or will) your anger solve anything, or will it only make matters worse?

If the consequences involved for your child are minor, then disengage from your anger and the fight. If your ex-spouse feels as though he or she has "won" a particular issue, then so be it. Often, the advantages of disengaging outweigh the disadvantages.

What your child needs most is for you to try to become a good "business partner" with your ex-spouse. Even though your marriage may have ended, you both remain engaged in the business of raising your child well. That may often mean picking your battles and keeping your mouth shut. You might even spare yourself aggravation (and raised blood pressure) in the process. If nothing else, do this as a way to love your child and seek to take the high road for that purpose. No matter how hard it may be, your ex-spouse is half of your child's heart. Drawing on that love and focusing on doing what is best for your child truly is the way to "win" in every situation.

You may even find other good things come from treating your ex like a business partner. I once gave a parent workshop on this topic, and later an attendee told me she took my suggestions to heart and decided to start giving her child's father information regarding their daughter's school activities. Previously she had intentionally kept him out of this loop. The father responded by cooperating with child support payments.

2. When you are ready, try to communicate constructively with your ex-spouse.

Your ex-spouse remains your "teammate" in a permanent sense. Given this reality, it is worth trying to find a way to communicate as constructively as possible with him or her. It's like needing to get along with a coworker you do not like or who rubs you the wrong way. Avoiding communication rarely helps, and this is even more true with your ex, where the matter involves your child.

Another benefit of trying to communicate constructively with your ex-spouse is that it provides your child with a positive example and reinforces the value of using communication when solving problems, regardless of the outcome. Constructive communication is one of the most helpful ways to resolve anger because it opens a dialogue, which can lead to greater understanding for both parties.

Here is an example that can be used to open dialogue when faced with a frustrating situation with your ex: "I'm feeling _____ (state feeling) because _____ (state what the other person is doing/not doing). I'd like it if _____ _____ (state what you would like to change)." Try practicing using this statement in other contexts so it comes more naturally when you need to use it in the moment with your ex-spouse. It is worth a try!

3. To help your child when she is angry, connect with her, then set limits and remind her to use an anger management strategy.
(For more on this, see Meaningful Connection Time #2 on page 108).
When your child is angry, she needs you to:

- Approach her from a calm state so she can regulate faster.
- Connect to her feelings and validate them.
- Set limits and provide guidance for expressing anger appropriately.

Safety, of course, is the first priority. If your child's anger has escalated to the point of cruelty to others or destroying property, immediate limits must be set.

4. Give your child control and choices when possible.
When parents divorce, much is happening in a child's life that is outside his control. Give him back some control when possible. For example, give him choices about dinner, the schedule for doing homework, or places to visit on vacation. Otherwise, your child may feel the only control he has is to make you lose control.

Meaningful Connection Time with Your Child

1. Help your child learn her anger warning signs.
It is important that your child be aware of her warning signs, so she can release her anger before it escalates and causes her to lose control. Ask your child to pay attention to whether any of the following warning signs happen to her:

- She feels hot (some children feel this in their face).
- Her muscles tighten, jaw clenches, or hands form fists.
- She gets a rush of energy; her heart beats faster.
- She cannot think unemotionally.
- She has an upset stomach or knots in her stomach.
- Her head pounds.

2. Support your child in finding and using an anger management strategy.
Helpful strategies include:

- Triangle breathing (breathe in for three counts, hold for three, exhale for three or longer). (Or, for smaller children, use "pizza, birthday cake" or "finger" breathing, as described on pages 67-68.

- Positive self-talk (e.g., "I can do this," "I will feel better soon.").
- Punching a pillow, taking a walk outside or in the hallway at school, or some other physical activity such as running or shooting a basketball.
- Thinking of a peaceful place.
- Reminding himself of consequences if he loses control (such as harming a relationship, getting a demerit at school, or losing a privilege at home).
- Writing out the anger in a letter to the person, then ripping up the letter. (Instruct your child not to send this letter, as that can create regrets and more problems in the relationship.)
- Talking with God about the anger and why she feels angry, expressing needs and expectations, and asking for God's help.

Encourage your child to try at least two strategies that work best for him.

Getting to the Source of Anger

Anger is considered a secondary emotion because it protects children from feeling more vulnerable emotions such as sadness, fear, helplessness, and guilt. Like us, children want to gain control, especially when feeling out of control, and they may resort to anger as a "quick fix" or an ingrained habit.

When your child is not feeling angry, help her get to the root cause of her anger. There are three root causes that underly anger: hurt, frustration, and insecurity. Based on your knowledge of your child, first ask yourself which of these causes may be fueling her anger. Is she hurt because of an unmet need? Frustrated because of an unmet expectation? Insecure because of a threat to her or her self-esteem? Next, gently ask questions to help her recognize and acknowledge this aspect of her anger. She will then be in a better position to heal this aspect of her personal wound related to your divorce or separation.

Helping her to perceive the reality of who you and your ex-spouse are as people is very important, especially as your child reaches adolescence. This is especially important regarding her nonresident parent, particularly if she does not see them often, or if she has a tenuous relationship with them. Knowing both her parents' shortcomings can help her appreciably in mourning her loss, healing, and moving forward in peace.

3. Talk with your child about having difficulties, failing, and making mistakes.

Is there a class that your child struggles with? Perhaps a peer is being mean to him, and he finds it difficult to assert himself. Talk with your child about his challenges, weaknesses, and mistakes, and what makes it hard to rise above them. Also, consider sharing a time when you failed and learned or grew from it, emphasizing persistence, openness to new strategies, and getting help from others. This discussion teaches your child that failure is okay and happens to everyone. It also lays essential groundwork for keeping anger in check.

4. Point out that personal growth is often a choice, but sometimes impairments get in the way.

Once your child acknowledges her own personal challenges in growing up, it becomes easier for her to accept that others experience these challenges, too. For example, point out that some people may give up more easily, ignore suggestions, or have low self-esteem that prevents them from taking steps forward. Also, discuss mental health impairments, such as major depression, that can make progress toward goals substantially harder as well. This topic can help your child develop empathy for others. It might also help her apply empathy to the parent who has hurt her the most.

5. As your child gets older, consider sharing information to help him better understand you and his other parent — including your part in the marital problems that led to your divorce.

The more your child can understand and accept his parents' weaknesses, the more fully he can empathize and, as a result, lessen his anger. The goal in this process is not to excuse a parent's bad behavior or wrongdoing, but to help your child put his hurt in the context of greater truth. This helps him see that a parent's action or inaction is about who the parent is, not about who the child is. This depersonalizes the hurt, reducing anger and putting the offense in fuller light.

Perhaps your child is aware that all people are imperfect. But does he understand how imperfections impact our ability to love others? Does he grasp that a person can only give his own love, not another's love? Your child's understanding will, of course, be limited by his level of maturity and cognitive development. However, it can be very helpful to plant seeds.

In my work with adolescent boys from divorced homes, I have often encountered many who were highly critical of their father's irresponsible conduct. These boys harbored significant anger toward their fathers for not being there for them or not providing financially for their families. Mothers in these situations inadvertently fueled this anger with their own, which in turn encouraged the boys to take their sides in the divorce. These reactions are understandable, especially in light of coping difficulties. But they can easily obscure truth and fuel lies of the Devil, who preys on the vulnerabilities of anger. When we listen to the lies, we get stuck in a cycle of anger fueled by falsehoods and half-truths.

As your child gets older, consider helping him break out of this cycle by:

- **Admitting your part in the marital problems.** This does not mean sharing inappropriate details. Rather, provide your child with information and guidance that he can use when looking to form healthy relationships of his own. Some examples:

1. "I let my job interfere in the marriage. Your spouse should be the first priority, but I made work my top priority."
2. "I married your father when I was too young and not mature enough to make such an important decision."
3. "I had some major personal problems during my marriage to your mother. I should have sought professional help for them, but did not. Those problems took a big toll on the marriage."

- **Sharing background information about your upbringing and/or your ex-spouse's upbringing.** Again, the purpose of sharing information is not to excuse actions or inactions, but to shed light on influences that contributed to them. This can make way for the healing power of truth to touch your child's wounds. It also fosters compassion and love for the "offender," which is particularly important when a parent is involved.

When I was a young girl, my father told me about how he grew up without a father. I forgot about those details during the rest of my childhood and adolescence, when my father was absent, and stayed engrossed in my own feelings, needs, and pursuits. As a young adult, in my quest to learn more about my dad as a person, I revisited those details with my mom. I learned that my father's father left home when my dad was a baby and saw him only twice, despite living and working a block away. While I could not fully appreciate what that abandonment experience was like for my dad, it increased my awareness of the considerable personal wounds that shaped my father and influenced his actions.

What the Church Says

Catholic teaching tells us that "in themselves, passions are neither good nor evil. They are morally qualified only to the extent that they effectively engage reason and will" (CCC 1767). In other words, it is how we act based on anger that determines whether or not we sin. What can we learn from the example of Jesus? We know, from the Gospel of John, that when Jesus went to Jerusalem for the Passover, he drove the moneychangers and merchants from the temple with a whip and overturned their tables. He said, "Take these things out of here! Stop making my Father's house a marketplace!" (Jn 2:16). While this story has a deeper meaning (emphasizing that the activity of the temple would be replaced by the risen body of Christ), it also shows that Jesus was angered at the corruption occurring in his Father's house. Granted, Jesus was perfect, and we are not, so his anger was very different from ours. Still, we can learn much from it and allow it to motivate us to delve deeper in discerning our own anger. Jesus' anger, which was rooted in love for people and hatred for sin, was righteous. Is our anger righteous, or are we succumbing to sinful anger, which is rooted in hatred of a person or revenge? We need to keep anger in check and ask whether we are being angry about the right things and in the right way.

To help children learn to control and work through sinful anger, it is important to reprimand when they submit to it. This means using appropriate, consistent discipline and not allowing guilt over your divorce to encourage you otherwise. If you think disciplining your child will add more struggle to his life, think again. In fact, not correcting your child condones his bad behavior and fails to teach him the importance of gaining control of his emotions so he can self-correct. In short, not reprimanding means enabling your child to his detriment. His anger and bad behavior will persist or worsen, and he will move further away from developing the self-control and skills required to live a happy, virtuous life.

Helping Yourself through Anger

Let's give more consideration to helping yourself through anger, since that is an essential starting point for helping your child manage hers. We know that suppressing anger is not a helpful long-term solution, as it causes anger to fester and explode later. As a result, anger can easily lead to immoral, unreasonable actions and, thereby, become sinful.

But how can we gain control of sinful anger so it does not lead to sinful actions? One way is to stop and shelve the angry feelings and situation long enough so that room can be made to understand another's perspective. Then, humbly ask yourself if the other person could have had an understandable reason for saying or doing what he did. Perhaps the other's action had nothing to do with who you are, but you are taking it personally or it is hurting you because of another personal issue. That, of course, does not excuse wrongdoing, but it illuminates the reality driving it which, in turn, can foster emotional healing. Trying to forgive the offender (something we often need to do over and over again) also helps, as does realizing that harboring anger, instead of forgiving, will consume more of our energy and peace of mind.

In this process, it is vitally important to remember that the Devil is waiting to prey on our vulnerability when we feel angry. The Devil loves to create divisions among us, particularly in our families. Succumbing to the Devil's lies and temptations always results in more pain and heartache. Instead, we need to make a conscious choice to turn to and trust in God, and God will give us what is best — including the grace and strength we need to act in mercy.

Thorny Situation

Your child's anger is chronic and intense

If your child's anger becomes more frequent, prolonged, and/or increases in severity, and your efforts to establish firm, consistent limits and rewards fail to help, seek professional counseling and/or a formal testing evaluation (e.g., psychological or psycho-educational evaluation). There are a number of diagnoses that may be contributing to the anger (such as attention-deficit/hyperactivity disorder, depression, anxiety disorder, oppositional-defiant disorder, etc.). As with any medical condition, the critical first step is understanding the cause of the anger so that effective treatments can be identified and put in place.

Questions for Reflection

1. How angry am I with my ex-spouse, on a scale from 1 to 10 (10 being greatest). Why? What could I do to support myself in reducing my number? What is my personal anger management strategy? What strategies could I try with my ex-spouse (such as opening communications with empathy, avoiding blame, or using kindness)?

2. How has my anger affected my child? What has been my child's reaction to it?

3. If anger has taken hold of me, how can I change my outlook so it embraces humility and charity?

CHAPTER EIGHT

Helping Your Child Bring God into the Solution

I had difficulty relating to God after my parents separated because I ascribed to God the same perceptions and feelings I had about my earthly father. In essence, I put my dad's face onto God. Because my dad was not actively involved in my life, I felt distanced from him — as distanced as the hundreds of miles that separated us. I did not understand why he did not initiate more contact with me, and I took it personally. I figured I must not be good enough, so I was not worthy of his attention. After all, he was a successful professional, larger than life in my young eyes, and I was just a kid who had not accomplished anything great. On a deeper level, I doubted whether my father truly loved me. That possibility was too painful for me to acknowledge as a preteen who needed her father very much, so I threw those feelings of neglect and rejection onto God instead. I concluded that God regarded other kids as more important and worthy of love than I was. While I knew I was a child of God and that God was a faithful father, I could not reconcile the difference between my concrete experiences and the perfect love of a heavenly Father. I could not fathom how God could love me when I doubted whether my own father really did. This, in turn, contributed to my feelings of disconnection from the Church as a child, even though my mother still required me to attend Mass.

Research shows that other children of divorce feel similarly disaffiliated. A study from the Public Religion Research Institute found that 35 percent of children of divorced parents are nonreligious as adults, as compared to 23 percent of children from intact families.[17] The study also states that those children of divorce who are religious as adults are less religious than their peers from intact families, as indicated by their attendance at weekly religious services (31 percent versus 43 percent). A major factor not explored in this study, however, is how the divorce impacted the parents' spiritual and religious identities which, in turn, impacted their child. If your child's identification as a Catholic has waned since the divorce and/or he feels distanced from God, questioning whether God loves him, it could be because he is observing these changes in you. Similarly, if he is clinging more to faith and the Church now that you have divorced, it could be because he sees you doing so. My parents' spiritual and religious affiliations remained strong after the divorce, and they definitely nurtured mine. While my mother's devotion was more concrete and my father's commitment more intellectual, I perceived them both as valuing and clinging to faith and the Church, which taught me to do the same.

Another key aspect is conversation, especially as children become teenagers. This is according to a study by the Fuller

---

17. Betsy Cooper, Daniel Cox, Rachel Lienesch, and Robert P. Jones, "Exodus: Why Americans are Leaving Religions — and Why They're Unlikely to Come Back," *PRRI*, September 22, 2016, accessed November 26, 2019, https://www.prri.org/research /prri-rns-poll-nones-atheist-leaving-religion/.

Youth Institute that is explored in the book *Growing With*.[18] The authors emphasize the importance of parents talking about faith with their children and continuing to discuss it in order to help them remain fluent. However, parents admit not doing so because they fear not knowing enough or saying the wrong thing. If that describes you, realize the main quality needed for these discussions, according to the authors, is a willingness to embrace them, not theological knowledge. The following suggestions can help you further.

Practical Suggestions

1. Share your faith journey with your child.
Consider sharing experiences of God working in your life with your child. For example, did you learn something from a homily that helped you grow closer to our Lord? Or did you ask a particular saint to intercede for you, then notice your prayer being answered in a particular way?

After modeling this sharing for your child, ask her what she learned during Mass, religion class, or in Sunday School that is helping or interests her. Allow your child to see you doing things at home that help you stay close to God as well, such as saying the Rosary. Your example can motivate your child to do the same. My father was an avid reader of religious books and newspapers, and he also watched religious TV programs often. It spurred my interest in these same activities.

Encourage your child to learn about a particular saint, perhaps one he is named after. Or encourage him to find a saint he feels could understand his struggles and trusts to intervene on his

---

18. K. Powell and S. Argue, *Growing With: Every Parent's Guide to Helping Teenagers and Young Adults Thrive in Their Faith, Family, and Future* (Grand Rapids, MI: Baker Books, 2019), 152.

behalf. One whom I have recommended to parents is Saint Raphael the Archangel. In addition to being the patron saint of young
people, Saint Raphael is the patron saint of healing in body, mind,
and spirit. If your child responds well to a particular saint, consider
buying him a medal of that saint and having it blessed for extra
protection.

2. Make Mass and confession a regular part of your life as a family.

Accessing the sacraments regularly is not just good Catholic practice. It is necessary to help your child deepen her faith roots so she
can persevere when her faith is challenged as a result of the hard-
ships with your divorce or separation. We know the importance
of good nutrition, proper sleep, and exercise for children's physical
health. We need to insist on similar, ongoing care for our children's
spiritual health and stamina, even if they refuse or put up a big
fight. For example, children must, by law, attend school. The same
nonnegotiable stance should apply to receiving the sacraments.

My mother required that I attend Mass with her each Sunday
and holy day. Even when I felt alienated from God, there was often
still something that managed to get through my resistance, grab
my attention, and stay with me during Mass. Sometimes, it was a
story the priest told during his homily. Often, it was my mother's
devout attitude of trust when she said the prayers and received the
sacraments. I knew full well that she was struggling daily with the
separation, yet in the midst of that struggle, she clung to her faith.
God was continuing to draw me closer and plant seeds of faith, but
I needed regular exposure to and nurturance from a faith commu-
nity in order for those seeds to take root and grow.

3. Establish a routine family time for giving thanks to God.

In the midst of struggles, it is easy for children, as well as ourselves,
to focus on what is wrong or not as it should be. As a result, we can
forget the ways in which God is still caring for us. Consider in-
corporating regular family time during which you and your child

acknowledge and give thanks to God for your blessings. You can schedule this "gratitude time" whenever your family is together, perhaps after saying grace before meals, during bedtime prayers, during the morning drive to school, or another family routine. The prayer can be a simple statement, such as "Thank you, God, for _____" (each family member takes turns sharing something he or she is thankful for that day). This habit will remind your child that God is still there to help him.

4. Point out the good in your family members and nurture those relationships, especially regarding your child's other parent.
To help manage the stress of divorce, some children split their parents into good and bad, seeing one parent as all good and the other as all bad. However, neither perception is accurate or helpful for children's healing and peace long-term. These perceptions can also add further difficulty for children in relating to God as a loving Father or to Mary as a loving mother. If your child is having this difficulty, try to point out and help him appreciate any godlike qualities in his earthly parents.

It can also help to instruct your child that the majority of human fathers from the Old Testament (such as Adam, Noah, Moses, etc.) were deeply flawed, but still encountered and knew God. Lastly, to provide an example of God's love, help your child nurture other loving family relationships. If your child is having difficulty with his father, does he have an uncle or grandfather who can provide some love and guidance? Similarly, if the difficulty is with your child's mother, does he have an aunt or grandmother who can provide extra nurturing?

Meaningful Connection Time with Your Child

1. Dialogue with your child about God.
Ask your child how he feels about God, especially now that God

has permitted the divorce or separation. Encourage your child to talk with God about this struggle and share anger, sadness, or other feelings he may be having. Reassure your child that God will hear him and respond with something helpful. For a concrete activity, please see the next activity #2.

Also, ask your child about his image of God. Does he view God as a loving Father, best friend, good shepherd, or something similar? Or does he view God negatively as a harsh judge, punisher, or the like?

For some children, viewing God as a trustworthy parent provides comfort when so much has been turned upside down as a result of the divorce or separation. However, for many others, it is difficult to trust in that loving image. It is critical that your child has someone to dialogue with regarding his thoughts and feelings about God and be permitted to express and process his anger, doubt, or whatever feelings he may have. Otherwise, children can easily develop an inaccurate and distorted image of God, as a result of the divorce or separation.

2. Do a "Giving It to God" activity with your child.
Another great way to encourage dialogue and nurture your child's spiritual development is through an activity I developed called "Giving It to God." I encourage you to do it and return to this activity whenever your child expresses sadness, confusion, and so on about a divorce-related situation.

This is how it works: First, you will need to get a picture of Jesus, Mary, or another religious picture, and tape it to a wall or other secure backing. Leave a couple inches of room open at the top corners of the picture, enough to create a pocket for folded-up notes to be placed in. You can also use a basket and keep it in front of a crucifix, if you prefer.

Ask your child to think about something that he, or someone he cares about, needs help with. It could also be a pressing question that he has. Then, have your child write a note to God the Father, Jesus, or Mary, or draw a picture about it, asking for whatever help he or his loved one needs. Next, have your child fold up the note or drawing and write his name on the outside. Ask your child to place his note in the pocket or in a basket in front of a crucifix. As you and your child are placing your notes, say a brief prayer like, "Dear Jesus, right now something in my life is troubling me or my loved one. I am placing it in your hands because I need help. Please grant me and my loved one your strength."

In about a week or two remove your notes and read them. Discuss what has changed in your lives since writing your notes. Perhaps your child's burden is not as heavy, or a nagging question has been answered for one of you. If your child does not notice a change, wait another week or two, then discuss it again. This activity will serve as a concrete way of reminding your child that, yes, God is listening. Sometimes, it might take longer than we want to get an answer, or we may get help in a different way than expected or hoped for. However, one fact remains clear: God is always with us, through the good and the bad. We just need to keep trusting and inviting God into our lives.

3. Help your child learn about free will.

A common response I have heard when running divorce groups for children is, "If God really loved me, why would God allow the divorce to happen to my family?" Understandably, children can have difficulty processing this question, especially when viewed in light of an all-powerful God and their perception that they have not done anything to warrant this "punishment."

If your child struggles to understand this, start by pointing out that God does not cause bad things like divorce to happen. But God also does not stop divorce. Instead, God gives us the freedom to choose to do right or wrong, good or evil and, in turn, act morally or immorally. Having free will, therefore, means that God permits bad things to happen. However, when they do, God "mysteriously, knows how to derive good from it" (CCC 311).

Explain that God can bring good even out of very bad things, and he invites us to be part of that process. For example, your child may have a classmate whose parent has died. As difficult and unfair as that is, ask your child if any good has emerged from the situation. For example, perhaps other families helped out by preparing meals, helping with errands, and so on. We see with other tragedies how heroes and heroines often emerge, and people do more to show their love of neighbor. Ask your child about, or point out for her, any good that may have emerged from your divorce or separation (or a prior hardship that she has experienced). For example, has your child become more responsible? Become closer to a parent or another family member? Made a friend with a child whose parents are also divorcing?

None of us, of course, can know for sure what God's actual reason for permitting evil is, but moral philosophers have offered insights on this topic. According to T. M. Scanlon, a professor in Harvard University's Department of Philosophy, "A world containing creatures who are significantly free (and freely perform more good than evil actions) is more valuable, all else being equal, than a world containing no free creatures at all."[19]

Most importantly, when discussing this topic with your child, remind him that we, as Catholic Christians, have the responsibility to use our free will in ways that result in good, proper choices. God gives us this free will because it is how we can become holy.

4. Explain that trials show us how much we need God.
Point out to your child that we all need God, no matter how smart or talented we are, or how many other blessings we have.

---

19. T. M. Scanlon, *What We Owe to Each Other* (Cambridge, MA: The Belknap Press, 1998), 17.

We also need God's help in every area of our lives, and trials like divorce emphasize this fact. The Church and her sacraments are there to give us the support we need on our journey toward holiness. And the beauty of striving toward holiness is that it also leads us to true freedom. "The more one does what is good, the freer one becomes. There is no true freedom except in the service of what is good and just. The choice to disobey and do evil is an abuse of freedom and leads to the slavery of sin" (CCC 1733).

What the Church Says

You have probably heard that, as a Christian parent, your home should be a domestic church, a "place where children receive the first proclamation of the faith" (CCC 1666). As such, it is in the context of family that your child will learn to honor God, pray, show virtue, and seek God's will. While a tall order, the good news is that you and your example can have a tremendous positive influence on your child's faith life.

Scripture tells us, "If my father and mother forsake me, the Lord will take me up" (Ps 27:10). However, if your child's experience of her earthly father or mother has been fraught with pain and suffering, it can be difficult to trust in these promises. I could not embrace them fully until after I had healed sufficiently from the emotional wounds caused by my father's absence. For me, the emotional healing fostered the spiritual healing and needed to be tended to first. Like your child's grieving journey, her faith journey will likely need to progress at its own rate. It cannot be drilled into her like a subject at school. Still, as a parent, you can plant important seeds by offering Catholic instruction and prayers.

God, Our Father

Throughout my childhood and into my college years, I worked very hard in school, trying to earn my father's love and affection. He already loved me, but I needed more than he could provide. My unrelenting pursuit of achievement fostered my denial of this reality and kept me from accepting this cross in my life.

It was profoundly healing and comforting when I at last learned that God's love is unconditional and not based on me having to prove myself worthy of it. Saint Paul's letter to the Romans describes this incredible truth: "God proves his love for us in that while we were still sinners Christ died for us. How much more then, since we are now justified by his blood, will we be saved through him from the wrath. Indeed, if, while we were enemies, we were reconciled to God through the death of his Son, how much more, once reconciled, will we be saved by his life" (Rom 5:8–10). We know that Jesus died for us when we were at our worst; we did nothing to earn his love. We can have peace and confidence that, in sharing in the risen life of Christ, we have continued access to God's love through the Holy Spirit. We will always be God's children.

Mary, Our Mother

As Catholics, we regard Mary, the Mother of Jesus, as our spiritual mother and a special model of holiness. The Gospel of John tells us that Mary stood at the foot of the cross as Jesus was dying. And "when Jesus saw his mother, and the disciple whom he loved standing near, he said to his mother, 'Woman, here is your son.' Then he said to the disciple, 'Here is your mother'" (Jn 19:26–27). John, the beloved disciple, symbolizes all humanity. Thus, from the cross, Jesus gave his mother, Mary, not only to John, but also to us. This means we can turn to Mary for guidance, protection, and assistance, and she will add her grace to our prayers to make them more powerful and acceptable to God. In addition to the Hail Mary, consider sharing other prayers in honor of Mary with your child, such as the *Memorare* and "Hail Holy Queen."

Thorny Situation

Your Child's Other Parent Is Not Taking Him to Mass

Some Catholic parents become concerned, understandably, if their child's other parent is not devout in the Faith. Perhaps your ex-spouse does not take your child to Mass or, even more extreme, outright mocks Catholicism and uses it as another battleground area, especially if they are having difficulty accepting the divorce, and they know Catholicism is something you hold dear. I heard of one situation where a divorced father became so enraged at his child's devotion that he took the child's rosary and threw his Bible in the fire. Nevertheless, the child remained devout and, eventually, found the courage to stand his ground with his father.

As with other values, rest assured that your example alone can speak volumes to your child. While you cannot control what your child's other parent does in his home, you do control what happens in yours. And your child will take note of what she sees. I was fortunate to see, time and time again, my mother embracing her faith. I also saw it making a difference in helping her face and grow from the cross of her divorce. Her strength and genuine love for God showed me there was something very real in nurturing a faith life. Keep on keeping on with yours!

Questions for Reflection

1. How has my divorce or separation impacted my faith journey? What would I be willing to try (or am I trying) to help myself bring God and the Church into the solution?

2. How has my divorce or separation impacted my child's faith

journey? Consider comments my child has made about God, going to Mass, etc. How can I respond?

3. What would I be willing to try (or expand on) on a regular basis to encourage my child to allow God to help her with the difficulties related to my divorce or separation?

CHAPTER NINE

When Your Child Does Not
Want to Forgive

As challenging as it may be, your child needs to be working
toward forgiveness. This is a goal that he will need your
support with time and time again. Regardless of whether you
think your ex-spouse (or you) deserves forgiveness, your child
needs to forgive in order to heal emotionally. Without finding
the peace in his heart that only forgiveness can achieve, he simply will not be able to heal.

After my parents divorced, my task of forgiveness revolved
primarily around my parents' fighting and my father's lack of
involvement in my life. I needed to forgive my parents for their
hostile fighting and not separating sooner, which would have al-
leviated considerable stress and fallout. I also needed to forgive
my father for not taking a more active role in my life after he left
home. As a child, I needed my father and deserved, like every
child, to be able to depend on his care and love, no matter how
many miles separated us. For most of my childhood, I also did

not know his side of the story, and my hurt deepened as a result. I stayed stuck in my grief for years and made little progress, if any, in forgiving him on a deeper level.

As a young adult, I became determined to find answers. Since my father was unable to provide me the answers I needed, my quest landed me in a health sciences library. After reviewing many videos of patients with various mental health problems, a light finally went on in my mind. I discovered that my father had a very similar profile to some of the clients being presented. I began to see him in a new light, not as a father who did not care or love me enough, but as a man with significant personal limitations, despite his brilliance and professional accomplishments. I realized, finally, that my father had likely done and was doing the best he could.

This empathy made it easy to forgive my father. It also helped me make more room for God within me, which, in turn, improved and deepened my relationship with my father. God gave me graces that allowed me to put my own needs and expectations aside so I could focus on learning who my dad was. I believe my father sensed this openness and acceptance in me, as he began to share more about himself and his thoughts and feelings on various topics. I learned that many factors contributed to the failure of his marriage to my mother (my parents later received an annulment) and hindered his ability to parent. In short, I did not have an irresponsible and immoral "deadbeat dad." Instead, I discovered a man who had significant personal limitations and was also burdened by unresolved grief over his own absent father. When I viewed my father only through the filter of my expectations and experiences, I failed to recognize the reality of his struggles. I also rejected the help that God was providing me to understand and forgive him. Forgiving allowed me to have an ordinary, day-to-day relationship with my father during the last years of his life.

I could not have achieved this closeness with my father had I not been able to forgive him. I also could not have learned the truth about who he was and, in turn, the many reasons why his marriage to my mother failed. I am forever grateful for these gifts and wish them for your child also. Every child has a right to learn about and understand who his parents are, parents who will always be part of him. Every child has the right to maximize the closeness of his relationships with his parents so he, in turn, can love others more fully, more deeply. While this may not be possible, especially in cases of repeated abuse or neglect, it is still critical for your child to experience the peace and freedom that can come only with forgiveness.

Your child will likely need your ongoing help to achieve these gifts. I urge you to read on to learn how you can help him achieve them.

Practical Suggestions

1. Process where you are in forgiving your ex-spouse and how you can move forward with this process.
The only way to help your child with the difficult feat of forgiveness is to get a better handle on it yourself first, both emotionally and intellectually.

It is extraordinarily difficult to forgive someone — especially a family member — who has wronged you, particularly if that wrong was intentional or even abusive in any way. The thought of having to forgive such a person, especially absent an apology, seems most unfair. *Why do I have to take the high road while this person has to do nothing and gets no punishment for the abysmal behavior? Moreover, how could the heroic action of forgiving such a person be helpful in the future?* Forgiveness can even seem like enabling, much like a battered woman going back for more abuse. The important thing to realize is that forgiveness does not do away with necessary boundaries. The Church asks us to forgive, but her teachings never require us to neglect these limits. Getting past this misunderstanding can be very helpful in forgiving your ex, or anyone else in your life who may need your forgiveness.

2. Model a forgiving attitude toward those who have wounded you, including your child's other parent.

Helping your child develop an accurate understanding of forgiveness will help him to forgive. However, we also need to "walk the walk." Make no mistake about it, your child will take her cues about forgiveness from your example. If she sees you digging in your heels and refusing to forgive, she will likely do the same. If, however, she sees you admitting anger and other difficult feelings while still trying to move through them and forgive, she will be helped tremendously. Your example will have the greatest impact on her.

Meaningful Connection Time with Your Child

1. Discuss forgiveness with your child and clear up misunderstandings.

Like adults, children often have misunderstandings about forgiveness. Make sure your child has an accurate understanding, so she has a better chance of forgiving her offender.

Common myths are (with clarifications to help you teach your child):

Forgiveness means excusing what my parent(s) did. It is letting my parent(s) get away with something.

It is critically important to begin this discussion by pointing out to children that they do not have all the facts regarding the divorce or separation, or a parent's struggle. Only God does. As such, justice for offenses must be left to God. We can be assured that God will take care of it. "I said in my heart, both the just and the wicked God will judge, since a time is set for every affair and for every work" (Eccl 3:17).

We can only focus properly on our response to the wrongdoing. Jesus showed us by his example how to bear wrongs patiently, which is one of the spiritual works of mercy. In the Stations of the Cross, we see Jesus falling three times while carrying his cross, and each time getting up and progressing to Calvary. As Catholics, we are called to practice this spiritual work of mercy. Although often difficult, bearing wrongs is possible with divine grace and asking God to help us carry our cross. We cannot do it alone. Additionally, when we let the Holy Spirit penetrate our heart and guide us, the wrongdoing can be transformed into something good. Thus, forgiveness is also a gift that we give ourselves.

Bearing wrongs does not mean we agree with the wrongdoing. Nor does it negate the need for boundaries when we are mistreated (see chapter 4, Thorny Situation, for a discussion of boundaries). Instead, bearing wrongs stems from spiritual wisdom that tells us that doing an evil deed, whether by what we do or do not do, will not overcome evil, nor will it bring satisfaction. The only way to destroy the sin and achieve peace is to bear the wrong patiently and with mercy. As we are told in Romans 12:21, "Do not be conquered by evil, but conquer evil with good."

If I forgive, I give up my power.
Children will not likely articulate this thought, but it can easily drive their resistance to forgive, especially given the imbalance of power that exists in their relationships with adults. Not forgiving can feel like one of the few areas they can control; it becomes an arena for acting out, much like not doing homework. As children move into adolescence, it can be especially helpful to point out what they give themselves by forgiving: freedom from the pain of the wrongdoing done to them. They are choosing not to let another's sin have power over them. Thus, forgiving is a way to claim power.

The offender has to apologize first.

In his teachings, Jesus does not predicate forgiveness on the offender apologizing first. When the person does apologize or show remorse, it can make it much easier to forgive and foster reconciliation (see next item). However, an apology is not required. The person who hurt us may never apologize, show remorse, or improve in their treatment of us. Often, when we insist on an apology first, we do so because we resist doing the difficult work of forgiving.

Once again, our focus needs to be on what we are required to do. As we recite in the Lord's Prayer, "Forgive us our trespasses, as we forgive those who trespass against us." Jesus is teaching us that God's mercy is unconditional and limitless, and we are called to forgive others in the same way.

We receive God's forgiveness through the Sacrament of Reconciliation, where we say the Act of Contrition, expressing regret for our sins, rejecting sin, and vowing to improve. We need to extend that forgiveness to others. Otherwise, we cut ourselves off from God. Viewing forgiveness as a gift to God, because we have been forgiven, can help us to forgive.

Forgiveness means having a close relationship with the person who hurt me.

Forgiveness differs from reconciliation. Reconciliation occurs after forgiveness, when the person who hurts us repents and we re-establish our relationship with him or her. Sometimes, reconciliation is not advised, especially in situations of repeated abuse or when the offender refuses to change. Reconciliation requires that both parties accept responsibility for working on the relationship.

In contrast, forgiveness is a one-way process and does not depend on what the offender does or does not do. When on the cross, with incredible strength and mercy, Jesus forgave those who had not repented. We are called to do the same, and we can, with the help of his grace.

In order to forgive, I need to wait until I am no longer upset with the person.
Forgiveness does not depend on our feelings or emotions. Rather, it is a choice we make regardless of how we feel. Because of our human nature, we may continue to be angry or upset with the person who hurt us, even after choosing to forgive. That is okay. Forgiveness is a choice that we often need to make repeatedly. When we do so, that choice will help the healing of our feelings and emotions, which often takes a while to achieve. For this reason, forgiveness can be a slow process.

In order to forgive, I need to forget.
Human nature does not permit us to forget situations that have wounded us, with the exception of certain traumas under certain circumstances. It is not the remembering that poses the problem, but the actions we may take based on our memories. Do we hold onto the remembering as an excuse not to forgive? Or do we remember in order to set appropriate boundaries with an offender who is unwilling to change and treat us with respect (or perhaps is incapable of doing so)?

2. Help your child learn about the weaknesses of her "offender."
As with the prior suggestion, this too can be difficult, especially if an offender, such as your child's other parent, has hurt you as well. The last thing you may be inclined to do is set those feelings aside in order to try and perceive that person's struggles more fully. However, the more you can stretch yourself to embrace this challenge of empathy, the more it will help your child (as well as yourself). In fact, this can help him in a major way, if you're willing to love your child more than you dislike your ex.

Catholic teaching tells us that "the first duty of parents toward their children is to love them. Nature inculcates this clearly, and it is customary to describe parents who lack this affection as unnatural."[20] When children do not experience parental love, they can easily take it personally because of their developmental level and need for their parents. However, some parents are unable to give the love they should because of their weaknesses, a mental disorder, and the like. Helping your child understand that a parent's failings are a reflection of who that parent is, not who your child is, puts those failings in the healing light of truth. This will help to lessen your child's pain and cultivate empathy, which will make the path to forgiveness much easier.

When Jesus was crucified he said, "Father, forgive them, they know not what they do" (Lk 23:34). Jesus realized the people who wronged him were flawed. This can be a difficult truth for your child to accept, but it can help her immeasurably and give her peace.

What the Church Says

In the Gospels, Peter confronts Jesus with a question about forgiveness. He asks, "Lord, if my brother sins against me, how often must I forgive him? As many as seven times?" (Mt 18:21). And Jesus answers, "I say to you, not seven times but seventy-seven times" (18:22). In other words, we are to forgive without limits and without conditions. The Lord's Prayer gives us the reason for this demanding obligation. We pray, "forgive us our trespasses, as we forgive those who trespass against us," meaning that the forgiveness that we receive from God should lead us to forgive those who have wronged us. God shows mercy to everyone, including those who intentionally wrong us, even those who are closest to us. If we truly believe that God shows mercy toward our offenders, then we must do the same.

---

20. "Parents," in Charles G. Herberman, et al., eds. *The Catholic Encyclopedia*, Volume 11 (New York: Universal Knowledge Foundation,1907), 479.

This dictate to forgive and show mercy, of course, does not mean your child cannot protect herself from an offender or, in an extreme case, end a relationship if necessary. It is critical for children to realize that forgiveness does not mean they are to accept abuse. We must teach them to utilize boundaries to protect themselves when needed. (See chapter 4, Thorny Situation on page 75, for a discussion of boundaries.) However, in the process of helping our children protect themselves, we must also help them set their hearts on developing compassion for their offenders.

Stress that what is most important is to try and try again, while relying on God to help. We need God's grace in order to forgive unconditionally. The Catechism clearly states this fact: "It is not in our power not to feel or to forget an offense; but the heart that offers itself to the Holy Spirit turns injury into compassion and purifies the memory in transforming the hurt into intercession" (CCC 2843). Forgiveness often does not come easily or readily. Like other high standards and difficult achievements, forgiveness can require many attempts and they may not quite reach the goal. Let your child know this is okay.

Thorny Situation

Your Child is Highly Resistant to Forgiving

Perhaps, after following the suggestions mentioned in this chapter, your child continues to be very resistant to forgiving. And it seems that nothing you do is making any difference in helping him become more open to it. It could be that your child is resisting forgiveness because he wants to hold on to anger and the "power" it may be providing, especially when he is feeling vulnerable. Try acknowledging your child's anger, or his right to be angry, then give him an opportunity to express it, if he chooses. Once your child feels heard, he may find it easier to let go of anger and become more open to forgiving or to considering its benefits. Honor his timetable.

Questions for Reflection

1. When I consider forgiving my child's other parent, what thoughts and feelings emerge? What can I do or remember to help myself forgive him or her?

2. In what specific ways have I modeled forgiveness for my child? (Consider what your child has observed you doing, such as giving second chances, praying for someone who has offended you, asking the Lord to help you forgive someone, etc. What could I try in the future to improve my example to my child?

3. Is my child having difficulties forgiving me and/or my ex-spouse? If so, what are those difficulties?

CHAPTER TEN
Helping Your Child When the Other Parent Is Absent

My father's absence was the most difficult part of my parents' divorce. The hurt and confusion it caused plagued me for over a decade. It also presented my biggest obstacle to getting marriage right. After my father left home, more than anything, I longed for an emotionally close relationship with him. His absence created a gaping hole in my heart. I felt lost in the world and afraid to venture out on my own. Something major was not right in my life and, in turn, in me.

According to statistics, a large percentage of children live in homes in which one of their biological parents is absent. Nearly 40 percent of children in father-absent homes have not seen their father during the past year.[21] More than half of all children who do not live with their father have never even been in their father's

---

21. Wade F. Horn and Tom Sylvester, *Father Facts*, Fourth Edition (Gaithersburg, MD: National Fatherhood Initiative, 2002), 15.

home.[22] There are no similar statistics for children in mother-absent homes, but reports indicate that the number of mothers who choose to leave their children is increasing. About a third of all children with a nonresident parent live apart from a biological mother.[23]

Attachment theory stresses that bonding to both parents is important for a child's positive emotional, social, and behavioral development. Thus, it is not in the best interests of the child to be alienated from a parent and have his attachment to that parent damaged or destroyed as a result of ill feelings between his parents.[24] Sadly, however, what often happens is that one parent vilifies the other parent, sometimes rationalizing it as helping the child come to terms with the truth about the other parent. However, the child's sense of security becomes eroded in the process.

Having grown up with an absent father and witnessing the effect this had on my siblings as well, I firmly believe in the importance of nurturing contact with an absent parent as much as possible, barring situations in which that parent has harmed or abused the child. The only way attachment to an absent parent can develop is for there to be regular, positive contact that is unencumbered by the parents' hostility toward one another. No parent has the right to take this contact away from a child. It is also vitally important to realize how detrimental such an action is to a child's healing journey.

Practical Suggestions

1. Validate that your child was born from love.

---

22. Ibid., 28.
23. A. O'Reilly, "Maternal Absence" in *Encyclopedia of Motherhood* (Thousand Oaks, CA: SAGE Publications, Inc., 2010), 696.
24. Damien W. Cordero, "The Breaking of a Family: Children in the Battlefield," accessed November 26, 2019, retrieved from http://www.personalityresearch.org/papers /eagan.html.

Children want to hear that love brought them into the world. Even after the divorce, once the dust has settled, children may ask their parents if they still love one another for this reason. Hearing that parents do still love or once loved one another is powerful for children because it affirms their intrinsic goodness as a person made in God's image. This is why bad-mouthing is so destructive; not only does it bad-mouth your child who remains a product of both parents, but the bad-mouthing also erodes this notion of being created from love. This is particularly true for children since they lack experience with romantic relationships, and thus do not have the context or maturity for assessing these negative exchanges.

Despite how negatively you may feel about your child's other parent, reassure your child that you loved her other parent, and she was brought into the world as a result of that love. You could add that there will always be part of you that loves the other parent because he or she helped to bring your child into the world.

2. When your child is ready, and if interested, allow him to contact his absent parent.

As mentioned earlier, children have a right to know and have a relationship with each of their parents that is unencumbered by the parents' strife with one another. Both elements are critical to your child's healing journey and, in turn, can impact his ability to forge healthy relationships. Even if your child says he does not want any contact with his absent parent, let him know he has your support should he change his mind, provided that safety concerns are not an issue, of course.

If and when your child expresses interest, help him get in touch with his absent parent. This is also a situation in which enlisting the professional help of a counselor is highly recommended so your child can be prepared emotionally for any contact and visit, should it occur, as well as processing the visit afterward.

After my father left home and moved across the country, I

visited him in the summer and during holidays. Those visits afforded me an opportunity to get to know him in ways that no one else could have provided. They also gifted me with the experience of hearing and seeing his remorse for having been absent and learning his side of the story. No one else but my father could have provided me with that incredible gift. It also gave me an opportunity to allow the Holy Spirit to work and, as a result, help me grow in empathy toward him. Even though these visits were often gut-wrenching, especially as I boarded the airplane to fly home, they played an integral part in my healing journey as they provided information and exchanges with my dad that I would not have benefited from otherwise.

3. Find healthy role models for your child.

If your child's father is absent, consider whether there is an uncle, grandfather, older cousin, a friend's father, or, perhaps, a priest or deacon who can step in at times and serve as a good role model for her. If your child's mother is absent, seek out an aunt, grandmother, older cousin, a friend's mother, or, perhaps a religious sister. Sports teams and youth organizations can also provide healthy role models. In addition to teaching gender roles, these adults can instill other values and morals and, perhaps, provide a healthy model of marriage as well.

Meaningful Connection Time with Your Child

1. Answer your child's questions about his absent parent, sharing more information over time.

Your child may have questions about his absent parent. Asking questions usually indicates a readiness to hear the answers. Respond to your child's questions honestly and as best as possible. As your child comes to terms with his own identity, the questions may involve personal details about the parent. Your child will also likely want to know why his parent left his life. This issue, of course, needs to be broached gently, given your child's developmental level and how much of the truth he is able to process. However, approaching this topic slowly, while sharing information over time, can be tremendously helpful. It will prevent your child from taking the neglect personally and processing it as a negative reflection of himself. Children often blame themselves in these situations since it can feel safer for them to think they are somehow in control. In reality, bad things sometimes happen that they cannot control. It is critical for children to realize that the neglect is about who the parent is, not who the child is.

Your child will likely need whatever help you can give to understand who his other parent is on a deeper level. This information can help clarify what may be preventing this parent from being involved in your child's life. For example, is the absent parent emotionally immature? Self-preoccupied? Does he or she have a mental disorder/illness? Substance abuse problem? Or did he or she experience a traumatic childhood?

When having this discussion, it is important to share the parent's respectable qualities also, when possible. This balancing of information is particularly important in early adolescence if the absent parent is the same sex as your child, as this identification becomes increasingly important as children develop their self-concept as a young man or a young woman. If you highlight only the negative aspects of your child's same-sex parent, your child can easily fear becoming like their absent parent in a negative way.

2. Teach your child about the redemptive value of suffering.

As the Catechism states, "By his passion and death on the cross Christ has given a new meaning to suffering: it can henceforth configure us to him and unite us with his redemptive Passion" (CCC 1505). Thus, when we join our suffering with Christ's suffering on the cross, we share in Christ's suffering and become more like him. This view, sometimes referred to as "offering it up," reminds us that we are not alone and helps us to accept our cross. If we continue to trust that Jesus will help us through our suffering, we will find meaning in it. Share this important tenet with your child while reminding her that Jesus, in taking on our humanity, knows what her suffering feels like.

3. Share an experience when something good resulted from your suffering.

Is there a time when you embraced suffering with courage and hope and something good resulted from it? Perhaps it was something important you learned about yourself or another person, a special plan that God has for your life, or another blessing that you may not have experienced had it not been for the difficulty? If so, share the experience with your child. It will strengthen his hope that his suffering can also be meaningful and growth-filled, changing him for the better if he accepts it, allows God and others to help him, and makes good choices.

What the Church Says

Mary, the Mother of Jesus

The Church teaches that "Jesus is Mary's only son, but her spiritual motherhood extends to all men whom indeed he came to save" (CCC 501). This means that Mary is, indeed, our personal, true spiritual mother, our heavenly friend whom we can always ask to protect us, to intercede for us, and to help us draw closer to Jesus. She is also our example of faith because she realized her complete dependence on God and had total trust in God's plan for her life. Instruct your child in this important tenet of our Faith and encourage her to ask Mary to fill in the gaps that may have been left by your child's biological mother. Mary also gives young women a beautiful example of a mother's perfect, self-giving love.

To foster your child's devotion to Mary, pray to her together for help and support. I especially recommend praying the *Memorare* together. It is a beautiful way to nurture your child's connection to Mary, and a very powerful prayer for help and guidance:

Remember, O most gracious Virgin Mary, that never was it known that anyone who fled to your protection, implored your help, or sought your intercession, was left unaided. Inspired with this confidence, I fly unto you, O Virgin of Virgins, my Mother. To you I come; before you I stand, sinful and sorrowful. O Mother of the Word Incarnate, despite not my petitions, but in your mercy hear and answer me. Amen.

God the Father

The goodness and love of God the Father can also heal the wounds caused by the absence of a parent. Psalm 27:10 reassures us: "Even if my father and mother forsake me, the Lord will take me in." This promise is also declared in Hebrews 13:5: "I will never forsake you or abandon you." Thus, we can rely on the fidelity of God. We can have faith in a heavenly Father, even if our earthly Father is not faithful to us. We can hope in the promise that we will never be left alone. Encourage your child to ask God to fill that hole in his heart that has been created by his absent parent. Praying the Our Father can also help your child heal:

Our Father, who art in heaven, hallowed by thy name; thy kingdom come; thy will be done on earth as it is in heaven. Give us this day our daily bread; and forgive us our trespasses as we forgive those who trespass against us; and lead us not into temptation, but deliver us from evil. Amen.

Thorny Situation

Your Child Refuses to Talk about Her Absent Parent

Some children shut down any communication regarding their absent parent. A simple, innocuous question can trigger the child's anger. The child may say something like, "I never want to talk with mom/dad ever again." This unwillingness to talk about the parent certainly is understandable, given the pain, anger, shame, and other distressing feelings that such a situation can evoke. This is delicate territory, to be sure. However, as a parent, you can still plant seeds, letting your child know that if she ever wants to ask you any questions or talk about anything related to her absent parent, you are happy to share. In the meantime, pray that God will give your child the strength to confront this difficult reality when she is ready.

If/when that time comes, enlist the help of a therapist experienced in this area so your child can explore this territory in a psychologically safe way. This work can be invaluable in helping to heal her wounds and correct faulty, negative beliefs that she may have bought into as a result of her parent's neglect. Doing this difficult healing work will help your child open herself further to life in the Spirit so she can become herself fully as God made her to be.

Questions for Reflection

1. What is my child's cross with respect to her absent parent? What has she found (or might she find) particularly difficult to accept?

2. What do I see as my role in helping my child find peace with respect to his absent parent?

3. What do I find challenging about this role?

CHAPTER ELEVEN
When Your Child Is Not Ready for You to Date or Remarry

I was very fortunate because my mother waited until I was ready for her to date. It took me a while to be ready, because I was very afraid that bringing a new man into her life would cause her to forget about me like it seemed my father had done. The thought of my mother's attention being taken away petrified me. I felt as if one oxygen supply had been cut off from me, and my mother dating would be another — and this one would do me in.

I could not articulate the source of my stress. All I knew was that I was not ready for my mother to make this change. I remember meeting the first man she dated. He seemed like a gentleman, but that did not register with me because I was consumed by fears and anxieties that the dating kicked up for me. My grief regarding my father's absence was still raw, and I overreacted to the dating because of it. My mother did not argue with me about the situation or try to convince me of her "right" to date. Instead, she put my needs before her own and stopped dating. It did me a world of good, because it helped me gain my emotional bearings rather than add to the emotional insecurities I was already experiencing.

I share this to illustrate the possibility that your child may have similar feelings if/when you start dating. Be aware that dating should not occur while a person is presumed to be married in God's eyes. It should be remembered that a civil divorce does not end the marriage covenant. It might be possible that a decree of nullity may be issued from a Church tribunal, which would declare that you are free to date and marry in the future. Yet even if you do receive a decree of nullity from the Church, it is important to remember that dating represents another change for your child and, as such, means loss. It does not matter what may be gained in the process. No matter how positive those gains, they cannot replace the loss for your child.

As a divorced parent who has obtained an annulment, you may be eager to find a new partner to share your life with. You may even feel as though your marriage was "over" emotionally long before the physical separation occurred. Perhaps you suffered through a difficult marriage for a long time. You may have high hopes for a new dating partner, and believe this person will be good for your child also. It is understandable if you desire to rebuild your life and find the happiness that has eluded you for so long.

The difficulty, however, is that children are often in a very different place than their parents with respect to their parents "moving on." Not only are children at a beginning stage in their grief journey, but they also have limitations in processing that grief as a result of their developmental level. In addition, children's feelings can conflict and be at odds with their parents' feelings and needs. Children want and need their parents to be happy, but they wish their parents could find that happiness together. Children are also struggling, often even more than their parents, with their wounds. It is as if they have just fallen off their bikes and have cuts, fractures, or even more serious injuries, and they want to get back up on their bikes and continue riding. They want to catch up with you, their parent, as you ride ahead, but they are not yet ready or able to do so.

Children can also struggle with loyalty conflicts regarding their parent's dating partners. This can result in an on-again, off-again type relationship. For example, it's not uncommon for a child to get along well with mom or dad's dating partner, but then not get along with this person if they marry the parent.

Practical Suggestions

1. Once you obtain an annulment, honestly assess if you are ready to date.
Even if you were the one who filed for divorce and pursued an annulment, be aware that you will likely still encounter some grief as a result of the changes and losses involved. Dating can seem like a good antidote for that grief. You may also be eager for a new start with a partner who will provide the love and respect that waned in your marriage. You might also be hoping to find a partner who will provide support for your children and serve as a good role model for them. These needs and desires certainly are good and healthy. However, it is vital to assess honestly if you are ready to embark on a new relationship or whether you are rebounding as a way of trying to numb or eradicate the pain. If the latter, it will not work and only create another upheaval for you and your child.

How long does it take before a divorced person is ready to date and move on to a new life? When a loved one dies, a common expectation is that it takes one year before the bereaved can move forward. In divorce, the grief can be trickier to resolve. In addition, there may be more changes to negotiate and adjust to with family relationships. Given both factors, being ready to move forward after divorce often takes longer than one year.

This, of course, also applies to the person you are dating if he or she is divorced.

2. When ready to date, go slowly.

Going slowly means waiting to introduce your dating partner to your child. How long should you wait? As long as possible. Why? Because, if the relationship ends, you will have burdened your child with another loss at a time when he likely has not sufficiently grieved the divorce and its accompanying losses. It is also wise to keep your antennae raised for how your dating partner feels about children and treats his or her own children because those attitudes will likely apply to how they perceive and treat your child.

If your relationship progresses to the point where you want to introduce this person to your child, it's vitally important for everyone to continue moving slowly. Accept that your child will be in a very different place than you are with respect to this person whom he is just meeting. Your child also likely has no dating experience, so he will not have an emotional framework for understanding what dating means and that it can follow divorce and getting an annulment. Your child can also easily view a friendship with this person as disloyalty to his other parent. Accepting the new reality of your dating can be complicated for your child on many levels. Remember, his needs will differ greatly from yours.

3. Accept that your child may have a very different perspective regarding your dating.

As an adult, you may be thrilled about having found a solid romantic relationship. You are filled with hope about it, including the good things it may bring to your child's life. However, your child's view is likely to be very different. Not only do children often view dating as "weird," given their developmental level and lack of experience, it often causes them to wonder, "Am I going to go through another divorce?" Children can easily grow resentful of or even feel threatened by their parent's dating partner, because they do not understand how parental and romantic love differ. And if, for example, they grow fond of dad's girlfriend, they may feel conflicted, interpreting those feelings as being disloyal to their mom.

I was an older teenager when my mom began dating again. Even though it was years after my dad left home, at the time, I still had difficulties accepting the situation. I viewed this man as my competitor, someone who would be stealing my mother's attention and love away from me, even though I knew nothing about him at the time. I felt threatened and also had no framework from which to understand how parental and romantic love differed. I could not understand how my fears were not stemming from the reality of the situation or from who my mom was. My brother did not readily accept my mother's boyfriend either. The first time her boyfriend introduced himself, he extended his hand to shake hands with my brother, who turned away and left the room. My brother took on the role of protector and was not about to welcome this new person so easily.

Remember, while you may have been dating this person for months or longer, your child is just meeting him or her. Give your child time, patience, and the freedom to sort through the confusing and conflicting feelings he may have about this situation.

4. If you plan to remarry, consider enlisting support and guidance from a family counselor.

Remarriage is often a difficult transition for children in many respects. There will also be a lot of new groundwork that needs to be put in place as everyone adjusts to this major change. There is no one-size-fits-all solution or set of strategies that guarantees success. What works for one family may not work for yours. A family counselor with experience in this area can help you and your children work through the specific challenges that you will encounter and strengthen communication, conflict resolution, and other skills that are needed in the process.

Meaningful Connection Time with Your Child

1. Let your child know if you are dating.
To protect your child from another loss, it is best not to introduce your child to your dating partner until the relationship becomes serious. However, it is also important to let your child know when you are dating so that if/when you introduce your dating partner, it will not come as a complete shock. As with other divorce-related changes that impact your child, it is necessary to discuss this one. The only way to help your child adjust is to give her permission to air whatever feelings and concerns she has regarding it. Talking it out reduces your child's acting out.

You should also inform your ex-spouse that you are dating, so your child does not feel as though she has to keep a secret, which would only put her in the middle. Your ex-spouse is also entitled to know this information for safety reasons, just as you are if situations are reversed, in the event this adult has contact with your child.

2. Reassure your child of the good things that are not changing.
It is important to remind your child often that your dating (or remarriage) does not and will not change your love for him. Elementary-aged children especially often worry that a parent's new partner will take away that love. Explain that parent love is unique and separate from love for another adult. Also, stress to your child that your love for them is forever, and nothing can change that because of the special bond you share. It is also important to remind your child that your divorce or separation remains a matter between you and his other parent. And there was nothing that your child did that caused it.

It is, of course, important to continue showing your child just how special she is. Try to spend exclusive time with her and make it part of your daily routine (for example, always spend fifteen minutes before bedtime). Be present to listen to her needs and concerns. Also during this time, remind her of other good things in her life that are not changing, such as your family outings (going to Mass, family vacations, visiting relatives, etc.), still living with siblings, and so on. This awareness can help to balance any upset she may be experiencing regarding the changes associated with your dating.

3. If you remarry, let your child know her other parent is still part of your family.

Your new spouse cannot replace your child's other parent, just as you are not a replaceable parent. Some well-intentioned parents hope for this, especially if they think the child's other parent does not provide sufficient parenting or serves as a bad role model. While a stepparent can become a close, supportive friend to your child, he or she can never replace your child's other parent. For better or worse, your child's other parent will forever remain a part of your child. The more your child can achieve peace and forgiveness with respect to that relationship, the better her chances will be of having a healthy marriage and parenting in a healthy way in the future.

4. Acknowledge your child's struggles with respect to his stepparent and/or stepsiblings.

While you may be encouraged about the prospects for your stepfamily, it is important to accept that this transition is often a difficult one for children. Research states that it takes two to seven years and beyond for children to adjust to a stepfamily, depending on the conditions in which they were formed.[25] Even if it's a good change, children can experience it as another loss. In addition, given the slower rate at which children move through grief, your

---

25. P. L. Papernow, "A clinician's view of 'stepfamily architecture,'" in J. Pryor, ed., *The International Handbook of Stepfamilies: Policy and Practice in Legal, Research, and Clinical Environments* (Hoboken, NJ: John Wiley & Sons, Inc., 2008), 423–454.

child may experience this loss hitting him when he has not sufficiently grieved the prior loss of your divorce. If so, the cumulative effect of these losses may make it harder for him to adjust, and he may need more patience, empathy, and support from you. The practical suggestions noted in chapter 2 (beginning on page 39) can be very helpful. Remember, it is also important to follow your child's lead with respect to the development of these relationships.

The following guidelines can ease this transition as well:

- Allow your child to call his stepparent by his or her first name. Do not ask your child to call a stepparent "mom" or "dad."
- Continue being the disciplinarian. Do not assign this role to your child's stepparent. A stepparent's relationship with your child will have the best chance to develop if the stepparent focuses first (and exclusively, if possible) on being a kind adult friend.
- Hold regular family meetings. Life can get confusing (or "crazy," as some children state), when adjusting to a stepfamily. Set aside a time when everyone can come together to discuss matters affecting all of you. This will reassure your child that, no matter what challenges you all face, you will get through them together.

What the Church Says

You may be wondering if the Church permits you to date if you have not yet received an annulment. First, the Church cautions that the decision to separate (or divorce) should not be made lightly. "Separation must be considered as a last resort, after all other reasonable attempts at reconciliation have proved vain."[26] Even if

---

26. John Paul II, *The Role of the Christian Family in the Modern World* (Boston, MA: Pauline Books & Media, 1981), 124.

you have already obtained a civil divorce, know that the Church still regards you as married because Christ himself taught that the marriage bond, which is forged by God, cannot be dissolved: "So they are no longer two but one. What therefore God has joined together, let no man put asunder" (Mt 19:6). This is why the Church does not recognize civil divorce as ending the lifelong marriage covenant. As a result, dating in the absence of an annulment is inappropriate, as it would have the same moral character as dating someone other than your spouse while still married. The Church stresses that this situation tempts not only you in an immoral way, but the other person also. Without an annulment, you are not free to remarry in the Church, thus the Church does not regard you as free to date (since the purpose of dating is to find out if marriage is viable).

If you want to date and remarry, only an annulment, obtained after a civil divorce, would permit you to remarry in the Church. This is because a divorce is only a civil proceeding. It does not end the sacrament, but only what resulted legally from a marriage, such as shared money and property. In contrast, an annulment looks at how the marriage began and whether the couple had what was needed to form a marriage according to God's plan. When an annulment is granted, the Church is stating that a sacramental marriage never existed. For more treatment of Church teachings about this, see chapter 12, What the Church Says, beginning on page 165.

Thorny Situation

Your Child Is Being Rude to the Person You Are Dating

Your child has the right not to like whomever you are dating. If this develops into rudeness toward him or her, though, be sure to set a limit right away, just like you would with any other discipline matter. Later, when you have exclusive time with your child, ask him his opinion about the person you are dating and let him share his concerns freely. Refrain from reacting emotionally and defending your dating partner. Instead, ask questions to help your child evaluate his beliefs. Then, let him know you will pay attention to his concerns going forward. The reality is that your child may have keyed into something that you have overlooked or not yet observed. Even if that's not the case, you will have reassured your child that, no matter whom you date or possibly remarry, your child's concerns will remain important to you.

Questions for Reflection

1. Do I honestly feel that I am ready emotionally to start dating? Or am I looking primarily to bypass the pain associated with my marriage ending? Have I done what I need to do to ensure I am free to marry in the Catholic Church?

2. What healthy relationships do I have (or could I cultivate) to help support me emotionally if/when I pursue a dating relationship?

3. What am I willing to do to help my child adjust more fully to the reality that I am dating (or getting remarried)?

CHAPTER TWELVE

Using the Divorce as a Teaching Opportunity Regarding the Sacrament of Marriage

There are many facets involved in teaching your child about the Sacrament of Marriage. Some divorced parents have shared with me that they feel ill-equipped to talk with their child about marriage because of their divorce. I say the opposite: All you learned from your divorce gives you an excellent teaching tool. It is from our mistakes that we often learn the most.

That was the case for my parents. I credit the success of my marriage, in large part, to all I learned from my parents' divorce and the motivation it gave me to get marriage right. I felt I had an added obligation to succeed because of the advantages the divorce gave me. I had received a very personal look at why a marriage fails and, thus, what is required to make it work. I felt I had even more reason to make the right choice, not only because of being Catholic, but also because of all I had learned from my parents' mistakes. I was determined to turn this negative into a positive.

Some researchers theorize that children from divorced families have a higher divorce rate partly because they did not learn important lessons about commitment. Researchers refer to this as an intergenerational transmission of divorce, which asserts that attitudes about marriage and marital styles are passed down from parents to children.[27] In other words, by living through their parents' divorce, children learn that relationships do not last and adults do not have to stay in unsatisfying relationships.[28] In addition, it is theorized that children from divorced families have compromised relationship skills because they have not witnessed healthy conflict resolution between their parents.[29]

However, an important factor neglected in research studies is the strong positive impact that a parent's commitment to the child can make in mitigating these effects. While I did not get to witness my parents working out their problems and staying together, I did benefit greatly from experiencing a model of unwavering commitment from my mother and older brother, Marc, toward me. My mother showed me daily that I was her most important priority. Marc also took me under his wing and protected me, much like a father. These models instilled in me the value of commitment and provided me with a real-life understanding of what it meant. I, then, was able to draw on that foundation and apply it to my commitment to my own marriage.

Another important facet of teaching is helping your child grow stronger in faith and as a Catholic. "We know that all things work for good for those who love God, who are called

---

27. P. R. Amato, "Explaining the intergenerational transmission of divorce," *Journal of Marriage and the Family* 58 (1996): 628–640.

28. P. R. Amato and D. D. DeBoer, "The transmission of marital instability across generations: Relationship skills or commitment to marriage?" *Journal of Marriage and the Family* 63 (2001): 1038–1051.

29. B. Laursen, "The perceived impact of conflict on adolescent relationships," *Merrill-Palmer Quarterly* 39(1993): 335–50. And P. R. Amato, "Explaining the intergenerational transmission of divorce."

according to his purpose" (Rom 8:28). Read ahead to learn how to use your divorce as an opportunity to strengthen your child's understanding of sacramental marriage and deepen her appreciation of commitment as she discerns the way in which to live her baptismal call.

Practical Suggestions

1. Show your child that he is still your first priority.

While there may not be one right way to raise your child, what is clear is the profound, lifelong impact that your example as a parent will have. Your child will learn your values by watching your actions. If you consistently show him that he along with your relationship with God is your most important priority, he in turn will be more apt to show that same level of devotion in his relationships.

2. Share your dating mistakes and/or wisdom with your child.

As your child gets older and starts dating, share what mistakes you made when dating and offer your wisdom regarding these experiences so your child has additional guidance. If the direction involves an experience with your child's other parent, you will want to share it more indirectly, of course, so your child can hear it.

For example, before marrying, my mother did not date anyone else besides my father. She also started dating him when she was young. My grandmother was very fond of my dad as well. At times, my mother expressed irritation that her mother encouraged the marriage so much. I learned that dating and marrying young was risky. However, given my mother's negative tone about the subject, that knowledge was clouded by the sense that I was a mistake, just like the marriage was. Your child may not even be able to hear the wisdom contained in your advice if it hits on similar wounds. Be sensitive to this reality and consider more constructive ways to share what you learned. If my mother had said something like, "I think it's important to reach a solid level of maturity before starting to date," that would have been more helpful. It would also have given me a proper focus: I needed to get to know myself, my values, and what God was calling me to do with my life before embarking on a dating relationship. That, in turn, could have led to a discussion about compatibility and other major relationship topics that would have maximized my learning.

3. When your child starts dating seriously, point out areas of incompatibility.

As you well know, the person your child decides to marry is one of the most important, if not the most important, decisions that he will ever make. Start this conversation early, before your child gets emotionally involved with a dating partner, and try to maintain an open dialogue about the topic. Some parents fear that having this discussion will push their child away or drive him further into the arms of someone who may not be right for him. However, like other areas of parenting, it boils down to approach. Ask your child open-ended questions to get him thinking. For example, "Going to church is important to you, but your girlfriend does not go. How do you feel about that?" Share your experiences (or those of others) to illustrate your point. If needed, enlist the help of a more neutral third party, such as a relative or counselor, to help start discussions about the topic sooner rather than later.

4. Push the pause button.

As your child reaches adulthood, you may be looking forward to her getting married because her boyfriend has a wonderful family or you really want to be a grandparent. However, it is critical not to add pressure. As my professor of social psychology at the University of Notre Dame told our class, "One plus one is either greater than two or less than two." The best way to arrive at the former is for your child first to learn how to be self-sufficient and happy alone.

Meaningful Connection Time with Your Child

1. Teach your child about healthy friendships.
A healthy friendship is a vital building block of a healthy marriage. Teach your child about the ingredients that go into a healthy friendship, such as:

- **Making sacrifices**. Good friends make sacrifices for one another because their friendship comes first. For example, if your child and his friend want to play different games or watch different movies, one may give up what he wants in order to do what the other wants, and vice versa. There is a mutual give-and-take with healthy friendships, not one person doing all the giving or all the taking.
- **Respecting each other**. Good friends also respect each other's feelings and do not say or do things that they know will hurt their friend. For example, a good friend does not share what you tell her in confidence (unless it is a safety issue) or say mean things about you to others. A good friend also is not possessive. She allows you to be friends with others.
- **Nurturing the friendship**. A good friend makes the friendship a priority. That means he spends time with you in order to nurture the friendship, just as one cares for other living things such as a pet or a garden. Otherwise, friends can easily drift apart.

Ask questions to get your child thinking about what he wants and values in a friend, and to help him understand when a friendship is becoming unhealthy.

2. Discuss marriage and offer encouragement.

Children from divorced families often wonder if they will be able to have a marriage that lasts when their parents did not. Children of divorce often tell me that they are never going to get married or, if they do marry, they will never have kids because they do not want to risk their child going through what they did. Their feeling of doom can be pervasive, causing appreciable anxiety about failure.

Help your child develop confidence by pointing out qualities in her that will help her be a good spouse, if that is God's plan for her (such as listening, loyalty, generosity, etc.). Highlight people to whom your child has been a good friend, including siblings, as those real-life examples may nurture her confidence the most. Spending time with relatives or close family friends who are happily married can also provide your child with helpful role models.

Also let your child know that, like any success in life, marriage requires a lot of work, sacrifice, good skills, and so on. Point out that her choice of vocation will likely be the most important choice she ever makes, so she needs to take her time and approach it with much thought, maturity, and guidance from God. Remind her that she can be successful in living her baptismal call if she relies on the Holy Spirit to guide her.

3. Discuss other vocations.

As you know, your child can live his baptismal call in other ways besides marriage, including consecrated life (whether as a priest, religious, or consecrated layperson). Teach him about these vocations as he discerns the way in which God is calling him. The Vocation Resources for Parents and Families noted on the U.S. bishops' website (usccb.org) and those noted on the Catholic Apostolate Center website can help you.

Emphasize that these states of life are also journeys toward holiness and happiness. The question for your child to focus on is: Which path will allow him to love best? Encourage your child to learn more about these paths. Here is some information as a start:

- **Priesthood:** A Catholic priest is a male ordained minister of the Church. Priests commit to a life of prayer and celibacy. Most priests minister in a parish setting, as pastors or assistant pastors, while others serve as chaplains in universities, hospitals, the armed forces, prisons, and other industries.
- **Religious life:** A religious brother or sister makes a vow of poverty, chastity, and obedience. They serve in various fields such as education, health care, parish life, social work, and the missions. Some religious orders are contemplative and cloistered, dedicating their lives to prayer for the Church.
- **Consecrated single life:** Somewhat like priests and religious brothers and sisters, some single men and women embrace celibacy while living in the world. They devote their time and energy in service to the Church and find joy in serving Christ in their everyday lives or careers.

What the Church Says

About the Sacrament of Marriage

Marriage is a sacrament that allows a couple to meet Jesus Christ in a unique way. When a man and woman make marriage vows, they promise before God to love and honor each other until death, no matter what difficulties they may face in their life together. In order to make such a serious promise in the way that God intended, the man and woman must be able to consent freely and with knowledge and understanding of the responsibilities involved in marrying.

Marriage is a special, lifelong covenant that allows a couple to grow in holiness. In the Sacrament of Marriage, God pours grace into the love between a husband and wife through the Holy Spirit. This grace helps them love each other fully and unconditionally, the way Christ loves the Church. The Church teaches that a marriage ends only when one of the spouses dies.

About Divorce

The Church views divorce as a deep wound to natural moral law and, as a result, to all family members. However, the Church also recognizes that divorce may be the only answer in some situations:

> There are situations (e.g., physical abuse of spouse or children, flagrant adultery, or failure of child support, etc.) in which divorce may be morally justified, either as a practical necessity or as the lesser of two evils. In other words, to sue for divorce may or may not be sinful, depending on the circumstances, and to live as a divorced person does not imply a state of sin.[30]

The Church also recognizes that there are innocent victims in divorce. The Catechism states:

> It can happen that one of the spouses is the innocent victim of a divorce decreed by civil law; this spouse therefore has not contravened the moral law. There is a considerable difference between a spouse who has sincerely tried to be faithful to the Sacrament of Marriage and is unjustly abandoned, and one who through his own grave fault destroys a canonically valid marriage. (CCC 2386)

The Church teaches that divorce cannot end a marriage. Instead, divorce addresses only what results legally from a marriage, like property or custody of children.

About Annulment

After a couple divorces civilly, one or both of the spouses can pursue a decree of nullity from the Church (often referred to as

---

30. Michael Glazier and Monika K. Hellwig, eds., *The Modern Catholic Encyclopedia*, revised and expanded edition (Collegville, MN: Liturgical Press, 2004), 236.

an annulment). The Church's annulment process looks at how a marriage began. If granted, a decree of nullity means that, after a thorough investigation, a diocesan marriage tribunal determines that something important was missing when the couple made their vows to marry. Their ability to consent to marriage was incomplete or defective. As a result, the couple was unable to form a sacramental marriage according to God's plan.

An annulment is necessary in order for someone to remarry in the Church. If a person remarries outside the Catholic Church, he or she can still attend Mass, but is not permitted to receive the Eucharist. This is because, without an annulment, the Church considers the couple as still married, even if civilly divorced.

If you obtain an annulment, be aware that your child may wonder if that makes her "illegitimate." It is important to note that "all children born of marriage are presumed in canon law to be legitimate."[31]

Thorny Situation

Your Child's Other Parent Is Not Following Church Teachings

As a parent, you may be concerned about the effect on your child's Catholic identity if her other parent is not following Church teachings. For example, if your child's other parent is living with someone but not married, will that undermine your efforts to uphold the value of chastity before marriage? For me, it did not. When I visited my father, he at times was living with a woman to whom he was not married. But my attention was on

---

31. C. G. Herbermann, E. A. Pace, C. B. Pallen, T. J. Shahan, and J. J. Wynne, "Legitimation," in *The Catholic Encyclopedia: An International Work of Reference on the Constitution, Doctrine, Discipline, and History of the Catholic Church*, vol. 9 (NY: Robert Appleton Company, 1913), 132.

my relationship with him, so this other relationship was, more or less, like furniture in a room. I do not recall it having any influence on my morality. If it did, it was not a negative influence, as I did not view it out of context. I could not say the arrangement was contributing to my father's contentment or well-being, or that he was better off for cohabitating. In contrast, I viewed my mother who was not cohabitating as leading a happier life and being more at peace. Again, it was the overall example of each of my parents that made the lasting impression on me. It may be the same for your child as well. (See Cohabitation of Other Parent section on page 24 for additional comments.)

Questions for Reflection

1. What questions or concerns does my child have about marriage?

2. What can I do to give my child confidence about making his own marriage work, should he choose that vocation? Consider the suggestions offered in this chapter.

3. Which Church teachings, if any, regarding marriage, divorce, or remarriage do I have difficulty accepting? Explain my answer.

CHAPTER THIRTEEN
Making Amends and Reestablishing Contact After an Absence

Perhaps you are a divorced or separated parent who lives far away from your child. Maybe you see her only during the holidays or summer vacation. Maybe it has been a longer time since you have had contact, perhaps even years. Unlike the "deadbeat parents" portrayed in the media, you want to make amends and be part of your child's life, but you do not know where to start. Or you may have tried, only to find your child or her other parent unreceptive. You may be unsure what is best to do and, in your discouragement and pain, have decided to stay away.

My father wrestled with this situation for years. After he and my mother separated, he moved farther and farther away from me and my brothers, eventually settling across the country. In his later years, he shared that one reason he moved far away was because he wanted to forget about the past and start over. He said he wanted to pursue custody of me, but thought my mother would be a better parent. He also questioned whether he was even needed as a parent. This, of course, was untrue. My dad also shared his struggle about wanting to be more involved in my life but, at the same time, not wanting to create more upheaval. He was concerned about how my mother would react to his efforts to be more involved and feared that, if she badmouthed him, it might only push me farther away. He chose to write me letters instead.

The letters helped me to learn more about who my dad was. They also helped me to look beyond my own perspective and realize the struggles that he was experiencing. From his letters, I learned over and over again that his struggles were profound and prevented him from doing and giving more. It was not what I wanted to see, but it illuminated the truth of who my father was, which I would not have learned otherwise. That truth, in turn, forged a closeness between us that likely would not have been possible either. It also made my path toward forgiveness so much easier.

I am forever grateful for those letters and that my father did not give up completely on having a relationship with me. However, I did need him to do more and wished he would or could have tried harder. More than anything, I wished he had tried finding a job closer to where I lived so I could have seen him more often and involved him in the ordinary, day-to-day times while growing up. Our relationship did not work out the way it could or should have. Yet as I look back, I believe my father tried the best he could at the time. And I thank God for that consolation, which I carry with me always.

I encourage you to persevere in trying to make amends with your child. Even if your child or his other parent is not receptive, they may eventually be more open. Even if that day never comes, you will at least be able to look back and derive some comfort from knowing you tried for as long and as best as you could.

Following is some general guidance. Consider obtaining the assistance and support of a counselor to help you with your specific situation. Most importantly, stay close to the Church in this process, remembering that "nothing will be impossible for God" (Lk 1:37).

Practical suggestions

1. Make an honest appraisal of how committed you can be to the relationship with your child.

This appraisal means asking yourself some tough questions, and it may require the assistance of a counselor to help you process them as honestly as possible. These questions are:

- Do you sincerely want and are you ready to make a positive change in your relationship with your child?
- Is your personal life sufficiently back on track in order for you to take on this serious commitment?
- Are you willing to commit for the long haul, even if you encounter resistance and rejection from your child and/or their residential parent?

If you can honestly answer "yes" to these questions, the next step is to determine the type and frequency of contact that you can realistically provide your child on a consistent, ongoing basis. Children thrive on consistency, and this is particularly important when it comes to your visits and phone calls. It is not enough simply to show up. You also need to establish a plan for contact going forward, honor it, and communicate it to your child. This will minimize the chances of her feeling left hanging in emotional limbo after your visits or phone calls, only to feel abandoned all over again. It arguably does more harm than good for a child when her parent has inconsistent contact.

I never knew when I was going to see or hear from my father again. It was excruciating for me to get on an airplane after having had exclusive time with my dad, because I had no idea when I would have that time or hear from him again. To be brought so

closely into his world and then pushed back out in such a pro-
nounced way was more than I could handle developmentally,
both as a child and later as a teenager. I felt like I was seated on
an emotional roller coaster and wounded all over again. Had my
father given me something to hold onto, specifics about when
he would next contact me, the transition would have been eased
considerably.

2. Put your request for more contact in writing.

Writing is a good means of contacting your child and/or her other
parent, as it provides an opportunity for them to digest the communication slowly, on their own terms. If your child is in high
school or older, you can contact him directly. However, for a
younger aged child, you will definitely want to include his residential parent in your communication, or perhaps write only to that
parent. Share your reason for wanting to have contact (or more
contact) with your child and apologize for your lack of contact in
the past, giving an honest, age-appropriate reason, if possible. You
can then ask for them to respond to you in writing, or you can
offer to call in a week to discuss the possibility of meeting.

3. Plan the meeting thoughtfully.

If an agreement to meet is reached, choose a safe, neutral place
that will give the other parent and your child ample freedom to
leave if needed. Be sure to consult with a lawyer beforehand about
any legal issues concerning child support, restraining orders, and
so on, in the event they are raised. Remember to proceed slowly
and be as supportive as possible, focusing primarily on what your
child and her other parent need to say or ask. The more you can
put yourself in their shoes, the more it will help. Also, expect very
little. Remember this is a first step that will, hopefully, open the
door for more contact in the future.

4. Expect to encounter resistance.

Whether you are looking to increase contact with your child or initiate contact after a long period of not being involved, realize that your efforts may not be met with open arms. You know your side of the story, but your child and/or his other parent probably do not, or they may not be empathetic about it. In addition, it is natural if your child's other parent is distrustful or ambivalent about your desire for contact, if your past actions or inactions have hurt your child and/or his other parent. Because of her experience with my father, my mother was often concerned that he would let me down.

It takes time to build trust and, especially, regain it. You may need to be more patient and work harder than you are expecting.

5. Be prepared to accept responsibility for your absence.

If you are able to have more contact with your child, know that your past absence may be frequently on your child's mind. In many cases, it will persist as an elephant in the room, a presence standing between you and your child, until she is sufficiently healed from it. When you are ready and your child is mature enough, approach this topic directly, gently, and in an age-appropriate manner. Do not expect or look for a response. Instead, give your child space and freedom to process it. This is a sharing that you will likely need to have over and over again, given the extent of the wound that it has created.

In his letters and during our visits, my father often apologized and shared his remorse at having moved far away so that he could not be there when I needed him. He also expressed his desire to see me happy despite his failings. While it was heartbreaking to know of my father's hurt and struggle, I was incredibly blessed that he had the courage to share these feelings with me. It fostered closeness between us and enabled me to get to know him as a person. It also made it easy for me to forgive him and aided my healing considerably. I encourage you to give your child a similar gift. It will help her appreciably.

Prayer for Shrinking the Distance

The following prayer is based, in part, on letters that my father wrote me, as he grappled with the pain of living far away from me when I was growing up. I sincerely hope it helps you in praying through your grief and drawing closer to God.

> *Lord, you know my sorrow and fear.*
> *In the Garden of Gethsemane, you cried out, "Father, if you are willing, remove this chalice from me; nevertheless not my will, but yours, be done" (Lk 22:42).*
> *Deep down, I hurt a lot, feeling that I have failed my child. When they have needed me, I wasn't there. As much as I would like to avoid this reality, I know I cannot do so and be at peace.*
> *Jesus, my friend, help me endure this pain so I may be led to understand God's plan.*
> *There's so much I want to say to my child, so much about them that I would like to know.*
> *I am always wishing I could be more of a parent to them, but I don't know what to do about this.*
> *Lord, grant me your guidance and courage as I try to move forward and mend my relationship with my child.*
> *Please help my child to forgive me also for the many times I have disappointed them.*
> *Lord, you know the pain of broken relationships. Comfort me in my sorrow along this journey. Help me seek out and receive comfort from others also.*
> *Jesus, there is no relationship that You cannot heal. I believe you love my child even more than I do. With all my heart, I entrust my relationship with my child to your everlasting love.*

Amen.

CHAPTER FOURTEEN
Enlisting the Help of Outside Resources

As a divorced or separated parent, you know how overwhelming it can be to care for your child as a single parent, whether it involves picking him up from school when he gets sick and you are needed at work, added financial responsibilities, tackling school problems, or finding your own, much needed personal time. In addition, the divorce may have resulted in losing support from your ex-spouse's family that you relied on to help with child care issues. The challenges can seem endless. Perhaps you are trying to resolve these issues solely on your own, including emotional difficulties that you or your child may be experiencing. You may be bogged down with embarrassment or shame or simply want to keep the divorce or separation as private as possible.

My mother struggled with shame, and it added more stress for me. It also shortchanged my healing. As a child of divorced parents, I thought of myself as damaged goods. Going to school and Mass and having to keep the separation and divorce a secret intensified the stigma. My mother was definitely a survivor and brought me up to be the same. We did not want pity from anyone. Nor did I, as a preteen, want a lot of extra attention given to me at school because of the separation. However, it would have meant a lot to me to hear a kind word or be asked, "How are you doing?" by my teachers. I needed them to know my situation so I could go to them for support. Keeping up the appearance of having it all together when our family was falling apart at the seams did none of us any good.

Your child may also feel alone. According to one research study, fewer than 10 percent of children from divorced families report having an adult speak to them sympathetically during the divorce.[32] Even if there is an adult for your child to talk with, like a favorite teacher, coach, or a school counselor, your child may not know how to raise the subject or may find it difficult to do so on their own. In my work as a school counselor, I have had students bring a friend along to my office when wanting to discuss their divorce problems. Other times, the concerns have surfaced in other, indirect ways. For example, teachers have approached me with concerns about a student's writing in class assignments. In one situation, a student asked a teacher for help with a friend who expressed suicidal thoughts. In meeting with the student, I learned that one of the child's parents, who had been absent for years, had expressed interest in reconciling, and it was causing the child major turmoil, of which the child's other parent was not fully aware. Children need a regular place to air their concerns and questions regarding the divorce, preferably one providing adult facilitation and guidance. Otherwise, their stress can easily build and become more difficult to remedy.

---

32. J. S. Wallerstein and S. Blakeslee, *Second Chances: Men, Women and Children a Decade After Divorce* (Independently Published, 2018), 13.

Practical Suggestions

1. Inform your child's school about your divorce or separation and any major changes associated with it.

After you speak with your child about the separation or divorce, inform his teachers and school counselor about it so they can lend support and assistance, if needed, to help him continue doing his best academically and socially. Inform them of any other major changes associated with the divorce, such as a parent moving farther away, working longer hours at your job, and so on. School staff can provide information regarding your child that you may not be aware of. For example, I worked with a third-grader who became highly oppositional at school after his father moved out. His mother thought the boy's reaction stemmed from anger about the separation. However, the boy shared that he was very upset about his dad taking the family dog with him. He was actually feeling relieved about the father moving out because his parents fought so much.

The only way that school staff can help is if you give information about your child's particular struggles with the divorce. Ask them to share their observations of your child and, in particular, to report increases in moodiness, concentration difficulties or frequent daydreaming, or any behaviors that are atypical for your child. On a practical level, the school also needs to know if you and your ex-spouse can attend school meetings together or if separate meetings are necessary. They also need to be informed if you are giving someone else permission to drop off or pick up your child. Conversely, if a court order forbids a parent from doing so, the school will likely request a copy of the order.

2. Respect the limitations of school counseling.

It is important to realize that school counselors do not provide long-term or specialized mental health therapy, even if they are licensed and trained to do so. Instead, school counselors serve as a temporary, short-term source of support when children are hav-

ing a bad day. They offer a safe place for children to land as needed. As such, school counselors provide a bridge to more formal
counseling services.

Stay mindful of this fact as well: Some children do not want
to talk about the divorce at school because they do not want to
get upset and possibly cry, then have to answer questions from
classmates about what is wrong or why they were talking with the
school counselor. If this describes your child, respect her right to
privacy. Also realize that a school counseling session may, inadvertently, do more harm than good depending on your child's
limitations. For example, she may find it difficult to collect herself
after meeting with the counselor and return to class and concen-
trate on classwork. School counseling may also confuse a child if
she is also seeing an outside counselor, blurring the roles of her
school counselor and her outside therapist. For some children,
school serves as a much-needed respite from the stressors of parental divorce. It can be the one place where they can get a break
from thinking about them.

If your child is not having difficulty getting through the
school day, reserve counseling sessions for after school with an
outside provider. An outside provider can also work longer-term
with you and your child's other parent in supporting your child,
if/when needed. Seeing only one, outside counselor can provide
greater continuity for your child as well.

3. Try to include your child's other parent in school conferences.
Involvement from fathers, in particular, with the child's school
and schoolwork has been shown to help with academic functioning. Children with involved fathers get better grades, are less likely
to get suspended or expelled, and appear to like school better.[33] If
possible, attend parent-teacher conferences with your ex-spouse.
This allows you both to receive identical and simultaneous infor-

---

33. C.W., Nord, D. Brimhall, & J. West, *Fathers' Involvement in Their Children's Schools.*
(Washington, DC: National Center for Education Statistics, 1997).

mation. However, if you and your ex-spouse cannot be civil when attending the same meeting, another option is for notes to be taken at the meeting and emailed to whichever parent did not attend, along with those who did attend. Schools try to refrain from having two separate parent meetings on a regular basis, as this can put a significant burden on staff, especially teachers who teach a large number of students.

Even if your child's other parent is a noncustodial parent, he or she still has a legal right to access educational information about your child, unless a court order or another agreement specifically revokes these rights. This information includes not only progress reports or report cards, but also school newsletters, open house invitations, and the like.

4. Get immediate attention for troubled behavior or new ways of behaving.

Early intervention leads to better outcomes. It also reinforces for children that it is appropriate to get outside help when needed. For both these reasons and others, it is wise to seek professional counseling for your child early and as a preventive measure.

When is counseling particularly warranted? It depends on the extent to which your child's developmental progress and adjustment are being interfered with. The frequency, duration, and/or increase in severity of your child's symptoms or behavior is an important guide. Overall, any dramatic change in your child's behavior warrants further investigation. For example, restless sleep can be a normal response to loss. However, refusing to sleep alone for months or having persistent nightmares may indicate a troubled response. Similarly, a lack of enthusiasm can be normal. However, if your child no longer wants to do activities that he previously enjoyed or shows marked social withdrawal (and this pattern was not present prior to the divorce or separation), you should bring it to the attention of a licensed professional. Other red-flag behaviors, of course, are the expression of suicidal thoughts or engaging in self-destructive behavior. In either situation, immediate professional evaluation is warranted.

5. Getting a physical exam for your child is also important.
If your child is displaying symptoms that are concerning to you, get her a physical exam to determine if a medical illness may be causing or contributing to them. For example, if your child is feeling tired more easily or her activity has decreased, hypothyroidism could be a factor. Your pediatrician can also provide referrals to mental health professionals who are trained to evaluate and treat mental health difficulties in children and adolescents, if needed.

6. Do not let stigma or cost stand in the way of getting counseling assistance.
We do not give children the option of not going to the dentist or doctor. The same standard needs to apply to mental health practitioners. Some parents avoid getting this help because they fear it will reflect poorly on them. If this describes you, cut yourself some slack! Divorce or separation is a major stressor to navigate and, like other stressors, an outside professional can do a world of good in helping you and your child better understand and adjust in a healthy way to the changes. Another benefit of counseling is that it provides children with vital life skills to draw on when facing similar challenges in the future. After all, none of us is born knowing those skills.

Cost for mental health services can also serve as a barrier, especially if your health insurance provides limited coverage in this area. If this describes your situation, ask your child's school counselor if she or he knows of private clinicians who accept sliding scale fees. You can also inquire with your local diocese about counseling resources. Counseling centers at universities typically offer sliding scale fees as well, as do nonprofit counseling agencies such as Catholic Charities. It is definitely worth inquiring about.

7. Permit your child's therapist to collaborate with the school counselor.

If your child is seeing an outside therapist or psychologist, permit him or her to speak with your child's school counselor to exchange information and discuss strategies. This dialogue can be very beneficial for your child's treatment for several reasons. First, the school counselor will have information and observations, either firsthand or reported from teachers, that may lend a fuller perspective on difficulties that your child is experiencing. These observations can inform the therapist's work and help when implementing strategies and other recommendations for home and school. The communication will also encourage consistent terminology to be used with your child in each setting. Equally important, it can help your child be more accountable, knowing all parties are working together as a team.

As a parent, you may be reluctant to permit this dialogue because you want some family information kept strictly confidential. If so, discuss your concerns with the therapist and know that specific boundaries on information sharing can certainly be established. These professionals understand the importance of protecting client confidentiality and are bound by ethical considerations. Therapists and school counselors serve in different helping roles, which can facilitate these boundaries as well. As mentioned, the former provide more specialized mental health services, while the latter offer a more general service that is limited in scope, focusing primarily on difficulties impacting your child's school day.

8. Consider enrolling your child in a divorce group.

Guidance or psychoeducational groups are beneficial in helping children work through divorce-related losses and learning skills to apply to problems associated with them. These groups do not provide therapy. Instead, they help young people identify and express their feelings, and learn coping and problem-solving skills.

Groups also have the unique benefit of normalizing losses for young people and helping them feel less alone. Whenever you have several children together who are talking and sharing, their feelings quickly become validated. That experience can also be very cathartic for them. Moreover, one child may be able to articulate thoughts and feelings that another child is experiencing but has difficulty verbalizing. Groups also provide children with a feeling of safety through numbers. This greatly facilitates their expression of feelings, and it often happens earlier than it does in individual or family counseling.

Research shows that children who participate in groups experience a significant decrease in anxiety, isolation, and confusion. They also experience an overall improvement in coping. And these effects are maintained over a two-year period, at least. Even if the separation or divorce occurred years ago, young people can still benefit from a group because, at every stage of development, they rework and process losses at higher levels.

If your parish or child's school is not offering a children's divorce group, suggest this intervention to them. My books for children and adolescents, available at www.faithjourneys.org, provide Catholic-based curriculum. I also have a leader e-guide available and provide training and consultation for parishes and dioceses in establishing group programs.

Meaningful Connection Time with Your Child

1. Give your child explicit permission to speak with an adult at school.

Let your child know it is okay for him to talk with his teacher(s) and/or school counselor about the divorce and ask questions, if he wants. School counselors, in particular, can be an invaluable short-term resource. Children often feel freer to share concerns and feelings with their school counselor since he or she is not evaluating their performance. This alleviates concerns that a child may have about disappointing or burdening an adult and can encourage him to share more as a result. Your child may be missing or worrying about you or his other parent, struggling with staying organized in moving between two homes, trying to keep the divorce a secret from his friends, and so on. These concerns can easily have a negative impact on his attention in class, and may lead him to withdraw from peers or show other behaviors that are uncharacteristic for him. In addition to checking in on your child (formally or informally), the school counselor can also recommend outside resources and coordinate parent meetings, so your child can be supported as fully as possible at school.

2. Talk with your child about counseling and support groups.

I have talked with many parents who leave the decision about whether or not to pursue counseling to their child instead of taking ownership of this decision themselves. Some parents may know about their child's depressed feelings — perhaps they have persisted for months, or maybe the parent has been informed of the child's self-regulation problems at school. Even with this knowledge, though, parents may still avoid taking that next step and finding a counselor, because they fear that their child may feel stigmatized by it, which they feel will only make things worse. This is a mistake, and one that could cost your child a lot, not only because her condition could possibly worsen, but also because she may miss an opportunity to learn vital life skills for the future.

It is critically important and healthy to let your child know that we all need someone to talk with at times about our struggles. Just like we see a doctor or dentist when we have a physical health concern, and it is not "optional," so it is important to see a mental health clinician for emotional difficulties or those affecting our inner, subjective experiences. Doing so certainly does not mean we are crazy! Instead, it shows we have courage and want to grow as fully as possible into the person God calls us to be. Sometimes this requires that we work with a professional who has training and skills to help us heal and develop in healthy ways. It also lets your child know that you respect his right to privacy in the sense that there may be some difficulties, including those in his relationship with you, that he would feel more comfortable sharing with a non-family member.

Also remember that early intervention is key, just as it is for other health problems. It helps your child to adjust and minimizes disruption in her normal development. The conventional wisdom "an ounce of prevention is worth a pound of cure" can apply here as well. Otherwise, coping mechanisms may develop into maladaptive patterns that not only become entrenched, but are more difficult to treat. Your pediatrician and child's school counselor will likely have good counseling referrals to provide you. It is worth the time to contact any referrals yourself and vet them over the phone, since you know your child best. Also, let your child know that you would like her feedback about the clinician as well. If, after a few sessions, your child does not seem to be establishing a good rapport with the counselor, let your child know that she can try someone else. You can even make this agreement beforehand with your child.

Making this same agreement with your child about joining a support group can also be very helpful. For example, let him know that you want him to attend the first session, then you both will evaluate afterward whether or not to attend the remaining ones. In addition to giving your child some control, it also gives him an opportunity to meet the other children in the group. This often has the effect of increasing a child's desire to participate.

What the Church Says

In his address to the members of the American Psychiatric Association and the World Psychiatric Association, Pope Saint John

Paul II beautifully stated the Church's position with respect to mental health:

> The Church is convinced that no adequate assessment of the nature of the human person or the requirements for human fulfillment and psychosocial well-being can be made without respect for man's spiritual dimension and capacity for self-transcendence. Only by transcending themselves and living a life of self-giving and openness to truth and love can individuals reach fulfillment and contribute to building an authentic human community.[34]

Practitioners differ in their respect for the spiritual dimension of the person and openness to integrating the religious beliefs and practices of the client in counseling or therapy. Before agreeing to work with a particular clinician, ask whether any religious affiliation informs his or her work and, specifically, if the clinician adheres to Catholic teachings. This information should also be noted in the clinician's informed consent agreement. One way to find such a clinician is through the website www.catholictherapists .com. Pastoral education associations, pastoral counseling organizations, your local diocese, and non-profit Catholic agencies such as Catholic Charities may be able to provide these referrals as well.

I pursued my graduate degree in pastoral counseling because of the indispensable role that spirituality, religion, and theology played in my healing and growth from my parents' divorce. It provided such strength and graces for me that I wanted my counseling work with children of divorce to include the same so that young people would have the best chance possible of healing and experiencing wholeness. The pastoral focus also resonates deeply

---

34. John Paul II, Address to the Members of the American Psychiatric Association and the World Psychiatric Association, January 4, 1993, accessed November 26, 2019, Vatican.va.

with me. It refers to the shepherds in sacred texts, most notably Jesus. "I am the good shepherd, and I know mine and mine know me, just as the Father knows me and I know the Father; and I will lay down my life for the sheep" (Jn 10:14–15). Through "careful listening, through sensitive responses, and with compassionate understanding, the pastoral counselor shepherds persons into a new grazing land, leads people to cooler waters."[35] The shepherd metaphor is, indeed, a beautiful one depicting the caring and nurturing relational experience that is needed for healing to occur.

Thorny Situation

Your Child Is Highly Resistant to Getting Help

There are many reasons why your preadolescent or adolescent child may be reluctant to meet with a counselor or therapist. She may not trust that the clinician will keep the sessions confidential. Or, she may feel uncomfortable talking about something so personal, especially with someone who does not know her. Often, children do not want to share about the divorce because of their vulnerability. They know it will likely be painful to confront divorce-related losses and problems, much like going to the dentist. Additionally, if talking about feelings and concerns is not typical in your home, that can also contribute to your child's resistance.

If your child's functioning and/or the specific nature of his difficulty has gotten to the point where individual or family therapy is necessary (see Practical Suggestion #4 on page 177 for more information on this topic), then you need to "take the

---

35. M. C. Blanchette, "Theological foundations of pastoral counseling," in B. K. Estadt, M. C. Blanchette, and J. R. Comptons (eds.), *Pastoral Counseling, Second Edition* (Englewood Cliffs, NJ: Prentice Hall, 1991), 31.

bull by the horns" and take your child to see a therapist, just as you would take him to a doctor if he had a sports injury or to a dentist if he had a toothache. You can also try telling your child that you need him to participate because you need help in getting along better with him or in supporting him more fully. This approach may make him more amenable because he would perceive that the onus is not all on him or, similarly, that he is not "the problem." Keep in mind that many clinicians are experienced with working with resistant clients and, as such, will know how to approach and overcome this difficulty.

If your child's needs do not necessitate therapy, but you would still like to facilitate healthy coping for her (keeping in mind that play therapy is most appropriate for younger children), consider a psychoeducational divorce group, also referred to as a guidance group. Your child may be more open to this option because a group provides more freedom not to speak. As a result, she may perceive it as safer and less pressured. A secondary benefit is that your child may make new friends from the group with whom she feels a special connection because they can relate to the difficulties of having divorced parents.

Questions for Reflection

1. Do I think my child needs counseling support? Why or why not?

2. What are my thoughts about getting counseling support for my child and/or for me, if I feel overwhelmed as a parent or have ongoing concerns about my child?

3. Are there any coparenting skills that I would like to strengthen with one-on-one support from a clinician? Consider problem-solving, setting healthy boundaries, improving communication, etc.

4. Rate from 1 to 10 (10 being the best) how well I have facilitated my child's growth in getting help for himself. Consider things like staying present when he has shared difficulties, empathizing with his struggles, instilling a realistic sense of hope, and protecting him from negative influences that may be causing him to doubt God's love. Explain my rating.

EPILOGUE
Finding Meaning

While reading this book, you may have experienced a myriad of feelings — perhaps worry about your child's ability to rise above the divorce, a sense of being overwhelmed by the demands of single parenting, and anger at your ex-spouse for adding to the complications. Growing from this hardship and finding peace and contentment for you and your child may not seem possible some days. It won't be easy, but it is definitely possible, if you depend on God and the Church as integral to the solution.

Jesus well knows the reality of your needs and those of your child. He also knows that dependence on God is the answer to them. As Jesus emphasizes in Matthew 6:26, "Look at the birds in the sky; they do not sow or reap, they gather nothing into barns, yet your heavenly Father feeds them. Are not you more important than they?" We can be assured that, just as God cares for nature, so, too does God care for us, as we are even more important in his sight. We can take deep assurance in the fact that we belong to God.

My parents' divorce and, in particular, the absence of my father afterward, have been the most challenging experiences of my life. However, these experiences also encouraged me to grow the most as a Catholic, profoundly strengthening my faith and appreciation for Church teachings and practices. In addition, it required me to adopt over and over again healthy attitudes about suffering and loss, which I was fortunate to have instilled by both my parents. This attitude boiled down to essential questions: What am I learning from my pain? Am I learning something that encourages me to grow and change for the better? Or am I learning something that encourages me to give up on myself and others?

There are, essentially, two options for approaching the crosses of life. One leads to meaning or choosing life. The other leads to meaninglessness or, essentially, choosing death. Meaningless suffering is marked by thinking, "Poor me. Life is unfair. I'm bad. I'm powerless." When children view suffering as meaningless, instead of accepting it, they try to dump it. They may act out toward you, others, or themselves by engaging in self-destructive behaviors. Meaningless suffering occurs when young people think of themselves as victims. They cling to helplessness and are negative about life and themselves.

Meaningful suffering, in contrast, is marked by growth. It allows children to move past that "poor me" attitude. Even in their darkest moments, they find reasons to be hopeful and to recognize that, although things are really tough right now, they have power and the ability to make good choices. They realize their hurts will not last forever. They look to the present and future as opportunities to grow. And they accept help from others. When suffering is handled like this, it creates greatness inside children.

How can you instill this greatness in your child? She will draw on your example first and foremost. Does she see you taking steps forward to establish a healthy new life for yourself as a single person? Are you able to find joy amid the pain? Are you discovering and utilizing your God-given talents to fulfill God's plan for your life and to love others more fully? Are you seeking out supportive friendships and hobbies that enrich your mind, body, and soul? Or, does your child observe you focusing on the glass being half-empty, often complaining, and harboring negative, hopeless, and perhaps even cynical attitudes toward yourself and others?

Greatness requires a team effort. We cannot get there alone. Most importantly, we need to rely on God as a vital team member in healing the pain of loss and encourage children to do the same while drawing on Catholic teachings and practices. Does your child attend Mass with you and see you reaching out and praying daily to God like a best friend? Does he also see you reading the Bible, Catholic books, and watching Catholic TV programs to continue learning about Jesus and Catholicism?

God's grace is always available. However, we need to stay open and cooperate with it. When we do, we allow God to transform us, even in the midst of divorce grief, so we may become more like Christ and help those children entrusted to our care to do the same.

Acknowledgments

First and foremost, I thank God for calling me to write this book and enlarging the capacity of my heart and soul in doing so. When this path became difficult or seemed too burdensome, God strengthened me to persevere in the hope of doing good for others. A debt of gratitude is likewise owed to the Church for her teachings on marriage, forgiveness, the fourth commandment, and many other tenets that grounded me on my journey as a child of divorced parents, and Her sacraments which gave me graces to grow from it.

I want to thank Our Sunday Visitor for giving me the opportunity to write this book and the creative freedom to write it in the way I felt was best. Special thanks goes to my editor, Mary Beth Baker, for her talent and expertise, and for being a joy to work with. Her high standards encouraged me to do my best work.

In addition, I am deeply grateful to those in the Church who have supported my pastoral care efforts, including all my endorsers for their generous consideration of this book.

Finally, I thank my husband, George, without whose love and support this book would not have been possible.

Suggested Resources

Annulments

Annulment: A Step-by-Step Guide for Divorced Catholics by Ronald T. Smith

Annulments and the Catholic Church: Straight Answers to Tough Questions by Edward N. Peters

Mending the Heart: A Catholic Annulment Companion by Lisa Duffy

When Is Marriage Null?: Guide to the Grounds of Matrimonial Nullity for Pastors, Counselors, and Lay Faithful by Paolo Bianchi

Catholic Healing Resources for Divorced/Separated Adults

Beginning Experience International Ministry, https://beginningexperience.org/

Catholic Divorce Ministry, http://nacsdc.org/

Healing After Divorce: Hope for Catholics by Susan Rowland

Journey of Hope Program by Lisa Duffy, https://www.lisaduffy.com/

Recovering from Divorce Online Program, DivorcedCatholic.com

Surviving Divorce — Hope and Healing for the Catholic Family, a twelve DVD series with guide either for personal use or as a parish program. Includes Catholic authors Rose Sweet, Dr. Ray Guarendi, Christopher West, and Father Mitch Pacwa. Available through Ascension Press.

Catholic Pastoral Care for Children and Adolescents from Divorced Families

Faith Journeys Foundation, Inc., https://www.faithjourneys.org/

Making Your Way After Your Parents' Divorce by Lynn Cassella

Now What Do I Do? A Guide to Help Teenagers with Their Parents' Separation or Divorce by Lynn Cassella-Kapusinski

Restored Ministry, https://restoredministry.com/

When Parents Divorce or Separate: A Catholic Guide for Kids by Lynn Cassella-Kapusinski

Catholic Pastoral Care of Families

The Joy of Love: On Love in the Family (Amoris Laetitia) by Pope Francis

Childhood Sexual Abuse

My Peace I Give You: Healing Sexual Wounds with the Help of the Saints by Dawn Eden

Coparenting

Co-Parenting Works!: Helping Your Children Thrive after Divorce by Tammy G. Daughtry

Dating

- *The Catholic Guide to Dating After Divorce* by Lisa Duffy

Domestic Abuse and Violence

Catholics for Family Peace promotes a coordinated Catholic response to domestic violence and offers many resources. http://www.catholicsforfamilypeace.org/

National Domestic Violence Hotline provides crisis intervention and referrals to local sources of help in all fifty states. Call 1-800-799-SAFE (7233) or 1-800-787-3224 (TTY). https://www.thehotline.org/

Why Does He Do That? Inside the Minds of Angry and Controlling Men by Lundy Bancroft

Marriage Help for Struggling Couples

How to Heal Your Marriage and Nurture Lasting Love: When Divorce Is Not an Option by Gregory K. Popcak, Ph.D.

Retrouvaille is a weekend program with follow-up, designed for couples with serious problems, including those who are separated or divorced. Weekends are offered around the country. https://www.helpourmarriage.org/

Third Option combines skills-building workshops, sharing with mentor couples, and a support group. It can be used for marriage enrichment or crisis intervention. Spouses may come alone. http://thethirdoption.com/

Pastoral Assistance for Separated Spouses

The Gift of Self: A Spiritual Companion for Separated and Divorced Faithful to the Sacrament of Marriage by Maria Pia Campanella

Remarriage

Remarriage in the Catholic Church: A Couple's Guide by Joseph
and Linda Sclafani

Bibliography

Amato, Paul R., and Alan Booth. *A Generation at Risk: Growing Up in an Era of Family Upheaval.* Harvard University Press, 2000

Blanchette, M. C. "Theological foundations of pastoral counseling." In B. K. Estadt, M. C. Blanchette, and J. R. Compton (Eds), *Pastoral Counseling* (2nd ed.. Englewood Cliffs, NJ: Prentice Hall, 1991.

Cordero, D. W. (2008). "The breaking of a family: Children in the battlefield." Retrieved from http://www.personalityresearch.org/papers/eagan.html.

Cummings, E. M., and P. Davies, *Children and Marital Conflict: The Impact of Family Dispute and Resolution.* New York: Guilford Press; 1994.

Cummings, E. M., C. Zahn-Waxler, and M. Radke-Yarrow, "Young children's responses to expressions of anger and affection by others in the family." *Child Development,* 52 (1981): 1274–1281.

Cummings, E. M., R. J. Iannotti, and C. Zahn-Waxler, "Influence of conflict between adults on the emotions and aggression of young children." *Developmental Psychology* 21, (1985): 495–507.

Emery, Robert E. "Interparental conflict and the children of discord and divorce." *Psychological Bulletin* 92 (1982):310–30.

Glazier, Michael and Monika K. Hellwig (Eds). *The Modern Catholic Encyclopedia.* Second Edition. Collegeville, MN: Liturgical Press, 2004.

Herbermann, C. G., E. A Pace, C. B. Pallen, T. J. Shahan, and J. J. Wynne. "Parents." In *The Catholic Encyclopedia: An International Work of Reference on the Constitution, Doctrine, Discipline, and History of the Catholic Church.* New York: The Encyclopedia Press, Inc. 1913.

Horn, Wade F., and Tom Sylvester. *Father Facts, Fourth Edition.*
    Gaithersburg, MD: The National Fatherhood Initia-
    tive, 2002.
Ihinger-Tallman, M., and K. Pasley, "Stepfamilies in 1984 and
    today: A scholarly perspective." *Marriage and Family
    Review*, 26 (1997): 19–40.
Jankowski, P. J., L.M. Hooper, S. J. Sandage, and N. J. Hannah,
    "Parentification and mental health symptoms: Media-
    tor effects of perceived unfairness and differentiation
    of self." *Journal of Family Therapy*, 35, no. 1 (2011):
    1-23. doi: 10.1111/j.1467-6427.2011.00574.x
John Paul II. Address to the Members of the American Psychi-
    atric Association and World Psychiatric Association.
    January 4, 1993. Vatican: Libreria Editrice Vaticana.
Nord, Christine Winquist, DeeAnn Brimhall, and Jerry West.
    "Fathers' Involvement in Their Children's Schools"
    (NCES 98-091). Washington, DC: U.S. Department of
    Education, National Center for Education Statistics.
    ED (1997): 409 125.
O'Reilly, Andrea. *Encyclopedia of Motherhood. Volume 1.*
    Thousand Oaks, CA: SAGE Publications, Inc., 2010.
Springer, C., and J. S. Wallerstein, "Young adolescents' respons-
    es to their parents' divorces." *New Directions for Child
    Development*, 19 (1983):15–27.
Wallerstein, J. S. "Children of Divorce: Preliminary Report of
    a Ten-Year Follow-up of Older Children and Ado-
    lescents." *Journal of the American Academy of Child
    Psychiatry*, 24, no. 5 (1985): 545–553.
Wallerstein, J. S., and S. Blakeslee, *Second Chances: Men, Wom-
    en and Children a Decade After Divorce.* New York:
    Ticknor & Fields, 1989.

About the Author

Lynn Cassella-Kapusinski, LCPC, NCC, knows the difficulties faced by children from divorced families because she has lived through them herself. Equipped with a bachelor's degree from the University of Notre Dame and a master's degree in pastoral counseling from Loyola University Maryland, Lynn is a Licensed Clinical Professional Counselor, National Certified Counselor, and an experienced Catholic school counselor. Her professional background includes conducting family, individual, and group counseling with children, teens, young adults, and adults. Through her Faith Journeys Foundation, Lynn provides Catholic pastoral care programs to help children from divorced families heal more fully and grow stronger in their faith so they may pursue their vocations free of the burdens of unresolved grief.